D0874123

What Others Are Saying About Don Corder and *Minding His Business...*

The way a church conducts its business is a testimony to a world that is always watching. Church business needs to be done with professionalism and transparency. In short, easy-to-understand chapters, *Minding His Business* shows us the way to conduct church business in a way that honors God.

—*Dan Busby*
President, Evangelical Council for Financial Accountability
Washington, D.C.

Minding His Business is one of the best books on managing ministry available today. It is practical and insightful, and it reflects years of real ministry experience. Don Corder keeps it real with a no-nonsense approach to getting things done in a ministry environment.

—*Dr. Jeff Greenway*
Lead pastor, Reynoldsburg United Methodist Church,
Reynoldsburg, Ohio
Former President, Asbury Theological Seminary

I have known Don Corder for over a decade. He is as wise as he is brilliant—one of the most effective leaders I've met in over thirty years. *Minding His Business* is a gift to the kingdom of God and a must-read for any pastor or ministry leader.

—*Jon Laria*
Chief Financial Officer, OneHope
Pompano Beach, Florida

If talk and good intentions were money, the church would be a bank. Spreading the gospel is a job to be done, not discussed with good intentions. *Minding His Business* cuts through the clutter and clearly describes how churches can be set free from a culture of decline to make the difference God desires them to make in the world.

—*Alan Didio*
Lead pastor, Encounter Ministries
Red Cross, North Carolina

Don Corder is one of the smartest people I know. His ability to see through the urgent to what is important, and then to accomplish both, is inspiring. He is the best manager of ministry I've ever met. In *Minding His Business*, we are given the unique privilege of looking through the eyes of a true master to see ministry managed with wisdom and expertise.

—*Brad White*
President, Iak Donors
Palm Coast, Florida

Don Corder is the real deal. In *Minding His Business*, he speaks truth to most pastors' pain. This book helped me and my ministry in so many ways. It is required reading for every leader in my church.

—*Matt Young*
Lead pastor, LifeChurch
Amelia, Ohio

The wisdom on these pages is invaluable. Every pastor, church planter, and staff leader should put this on his must-read list.

—*Ronnie Harrison*
Pastor, The Kingdom Center Church
Louisville, Kentucky

Yes! *Minding His Business* should be required reading for pastors everywhere. Young or old, pastors will find truth on these pages that will make their ministries easier to manage and more effective.

—*Matt Wright*
Senior pastor, Water's Edge Church
Mason, Ohio

Minding His Business is unlike any other ministry management book I've read. The book illustrates business principles in short, easy-to-understand chapters that help me lead my ministry right now.
—*Michael Phillips*
Senior pastor, Kingdom Life Church
Baltimore, Maryland

The twenty-first-century church is a different proposition from its twentieth-century counterpart. The message is unchanged, but the methods are in a state of flux. Many modern pastors are expected to be spiritual leaders, platform talents, marketing experts, and CEOs. Where does one go to be trained for all that? *Minding His Business* is a gift to pastors who are struggling to serve their ministries as spiritual leaders and business managers.
—*Dr. Mark Smith*
President, Ohio Christian University
Circleville, Ohio

Having had the privilege of serving as Don Corder's pastor in the past, I can attest to his love for the church and for Christian ministers. *Minding His Business* imparts page after page of practical, useful advice. The wisdom found in this book will help pastors to manage the business of their ministries more efficiently. I wish that this book had been available when I was starting out in ministry thirty-five years ago!
—*Dr. Ken Alford*
Senior pastor, Crossroads Baptist Church
Valdosta, Georgia

This book makes sense. I would be surprised if any pastor or ministry leader read it and did not see his or her ministry on the pages.
—*Steve Howard*
President, Centerpoint Interactive, Inc.
Columbus, Ohio

In a Christian university, we work to integrate faith and learning on subjects ranging from science to literature, from psychology to technology. Unfortunately, we don't talk enough about the integration of faith and administration. Through Don Corder's rich experience and practical illustrations, his new book, *Minding His Business*, is a living example of that kind of integration. If thinking "Christianly" about administrative ministry is important to you, you will love this book.

—*Don Meyer*
President, University of Valley Forge
Valley Forge, Pennsylvania

There could not be a timelier book to hit the church world than *Minding His Business*. Don will lighten your load and elevate your life's work as you apply the practical "how to's" of effective ministry leadership.

—*Harvey A. Hook*
Founder, Relā
Columbus, Ohio

The stuff in this book really works! I've had the privilege and honor of working with Don in a ministry setting. He is an agent of change. He finds value where you wouldn't think it was possible. He has worked with people in the ministry to change the culture in positive ways, and the changes have stuck! Don's been there; he walks the talk, and he practices what you will read about in *Minding His Business*.

—*Eric Walton*
President, PL Coaches
Phoenix, Arizona

Page after page of solutions to the problems churches face when trying to execute pastoral vision. I highly recommend this book.

—*Jon Ferguson*
Senior pastor, Stillwater Church
Dayton, Ohio

MINDING
HIS
BUSINESS

DON CORDER

WHITAKER
HOUSE

MINDING HIS BUSINESS:
40 DAYS TO BETTER CHURCH MANAGEMENT

www.TheProvisumGroup.com
DCorder@TheProvisumGroup.com

ISBN: 978-1-62911-610-5
eBook ISBN: 978-1-62911-611-2
Printed in the United States of America
© 2015 by Don Corder

Whitaker House
1030 Hunt Valley Circle
New Kensington, PA 15068
www.whitakerhouse.com

Library of Congress Cataloging-in-Publication Data (Pending)

1 2 3 4 5 6 7 8 9 10 11 **W** 22 21 20 19 18 17 16 15

DEDICATION

TO THE "CALLED ONES"

This book is dedicated to all the people who have faithfully answered God's call to lay down their lives in service to the King by pastoring His people and leading His church. One of the greatest men of God I ever met, a pastor for over forty years, gave me a pearl of wisdom. I was in his office, describing a difficult problem for which there were only painful solutions. He listened patiently, then said, "Don, when you have a stone in your shoe, no one knows better than you that you have a stone in your shoe. Who do you think is worthy of greater honor? The guy who tells you that you have a stone in your shoe, or the guy who removes the stone from your shoe?"

That was the moment I first heard God's call on my life to ease the burden of every pastor and ministry leader I can by helping him or her conduct the business of the church. This book is intended to assist pastors and ministry leaders in "keeping the stones out of their shoes." I have spent most of my adult life helping others get things done while avoiding pitfalls along the way. When I worked in the business sector, everyone was of like mind, and keeping score was simple: satisfy the customer, make money, and do it ethically. But once I started working in ministry, conducting business became more of a challenge. Business and ministry may seem incompatible; but the truth is that the business of ministry can be done, and done well.

My hope for this book is that it will, in some way, help you to become more effective in what God has called you to do, so that more people hear the gospel and are transformed by it.

—*Don Corder*

CONTENTS

FOREWORD

The Battle of Yarmouk in August of 636 fundamentally changed world history. The forces of Islam came against the armies of the Byzantine Empire and its Western allies in the northern areas of modern Iraq. The Byzantine allies were marked by infighting, mismanaged supply lines, and poor preparation. The result was the first major victory for Islam. That defeat of the West over 1400 years ago is still the nexus for many of the issues in Iraq and the Middle East. It has spilled across every part of the globe, affecting our lives to this day.

Similarly, the decisions made by church leaders and staffers affect their ministries and the lives they touch for years and years. A friend of mine served jail time for mistakes his mom had made in filling out forms. Another friend made an uninformed decision and lost her tax-exempt status. A pastor friend struggles under the scrutiny of tax authorities as his church undergoes expensive audits every year for mistakes made by a staffer who has long been let go.

Don Corder's *Minding His Business* may not change world history, but it could very well change the history of your impact on the world. Don's wealth of wisdom and hard-earned experience, when heeded, is sure to make nonprofit operations safer and less problematic. We have engaged him to help administrate our own ministry, and his concise methods of planning and follow-through, along with the work of his experienced "shared" staff to integrate our systems, streamlined our operations, saving us thousands of dollars and enabling us to run strong with full confidence.

What you will appreciate in *Minding His Business* is Don's overarching desire for you to be successful—because, if you're successful, more people will meet Jesus. That's the *real* bottom line, and Don is always about the bottom line.

I don't give advice, but I will share some wisdom with you: Do what this book says. Don't merely skim and move on. Read it, do it, and win victories for the kingdom.

—*Paul Louis Cole*
President, Christian Men's Network

PREFACE

M*inding His Business* was written to make the lives of pastors and ministry leaders easier by providing pragmatic steps toward executing vision, making things happen, and getting things done effectively and with wisdom. In the pages that follow, I've written candidly about some of the most embarrassing, frightening, disastrous, encouraging, and enlightening situations that I have witnessed in Christian churches and ministries. However, no reader—not even my wife—will ever be able to identify the people I've written about. And I will never tell. These vignettes have been thoroughly scrubbed and fictionalized so as to protect the innocent as well as the guilty. But the essence of what occurred is absolutely and completely accurate.

If you seem to recognize yourself somewhere in these pages, it is only an indication that your problems are not unique, that you are not alone. After thirty-plus years in leadership, I have come to the conclusion that there are very few "new problems," just new people having the "same old problems," usually for the same reasons, and often solved using similar solutions. As entertaining or appalling as certain of these stories may be, they very well could happen to you. Stay in ministry long enough, and some of them probably will.

When a church needs a lawyer, it hires a lawyer. When a church needs a plumber, it hires a plumber. But when a church needs to conduct business, it often calls a butcher, a baker, a mechanic, and a stay-at-home mom to form a committee that takes a month to approve the purchase of a gallon of paint so that a staff member may apply a fresh coat of paint to a door in the nursery. And if the job goes badly, who shoulders the blame? The pastor.

Chances are, if you work in a church, you are not an experienced businessperson, nor should you be. God called you into ministry to love people into heaven, to support people through their suffering, to feed the hungry, to clothe the naked, and to take the gospel to the ends of the earth. You wouldn't hire an accountant to lead worship. You wouldn't hire a Wall Street banker to run your nursery. So then, why does the church ask so many pastors and ministers to manage church business?

One of the first offices Jesus set up in His ministry was that of administration and operations. We read about it in the Luke 9, where the feeding of the five thousand is recorded. Thousands of hungry people had gathered to hear Jesus preach, and now the sun was going down. There was very little food, and even less money. He said to His disciples, *"You give them something to eat"* (Luke 9:13). Someone had to figure out how to feed all these people, not to mention how to pay for it.

Jesus solved that one for them, miraculously multiplying five loaves of bread and two fish. But, if we are being honest, the church has been struggling to execute spiritual vision ever since.

One of the best ways to learn is through our own failures; almost equally effective are the lessons learned from the failures of others. Experience is what you learn from your own mistakes. Wisdom is what you learn from the mistakes of others.

Airline pilots follow rules that are "written in blood," meaning they were recorded based on fatal mistakes so that other pilots might avoid errors that might cost them their lives. In the same way, by following the principles contained in this book, churches and ministries can avoid crushing lawsuits, the perils of shrinking congregations, the agony of false employment claims, the pain of shrinking revenue, and other pitfalls. Maybe some ministry staffs will even have time and energy left over to grow, prosper, change lives, and spread the good news that will send a few more people to heaven.

I once worked with a ministry that had started with one man and grew into a megachurch. The pastor was driven and smart— probably one of the smartest people I ever met. Whenever he was asked how he'd managed to build such a huge ministry, he would answer, "By executing vision." He would go on to say, "A brilliant idea is worth a nickel. Executing that idea and turning it into reality is where kingdom value is created." This pastor understood that talk was cheap. He knew that a ministry that talks more than it achieves will struggle to grow.

There is a saying among operational executives that goes, "No job is too hard for the guy who doesn't have to do it." Surely, we can see the simple truth conveyed by those words. In this context, these words seem practical and true. But speak them to a person who is passionately advocating a big vision with grand ideas, and those same words can seem harsh and insensitive. Context is everything. And context was the toughest challenge I faced while writing *Minding His Business*. As I wrote this book, I struggled with wording each exhortation in a way that would ring practical and true, without coming across as harsh and insensitive. My goal was to speak the truth in love, as Paul exhorts believers to do in Ephesians 4:15.

While most spiritual vision is inspired by God in the heart of a pastor or ministry leader, the execution of that vision is mostly done in the natural—a process that's replete with physical, financial, and human constraints. It is from decades of successfully executing and implementing vision in spite of these constraints that I gained the pragmatic and candid perspective I offer in this book. Throughout its pages, I challenge the reader to risk having his ego bruised a time or two, as an "investment" in the greater good and an important step in his pursuit of the Great Commission. It is no mistake that the first two chapters are titled "'Price' Is Not the Same as 'Cost'" and "Nothing Moves Without Friction."

By offering a pragmatic and candid perspective on executing and implementing the business of the church, my hope is to facilitate easier decision making and improved outcomes. May God bless you and your ministry as you mind His business.

—*Don Corder*

INTRODUCTION:
CATCH THE VISION OF
THE "CALLED ONES"

The mission of the church is to make disciples. (See, for example, Matthew 28:16–20.) To facilitate that mission, God has equipped each Christian to do the work of the ministry in a unique, specific way. And He has called out a particular group of people to build or to lead churches and ministries, whether as pastors, executive directors, presidents, speakers, authors, musicians, missionaries, principals, or another role.

These "called ones" are often labeled "crazy" by other people. Noah's contemporaries surely didn't understand what he was doing when he started constructing a massive ark in the middle of the desert. And even Jesus' closest friends tried to talk him out of many of the things He did. The "called ones" care far more about serving people than about conducting business, and so should we.

"Called ones" are walking with an omnipotent God who always takes each ministry—as He takes each individual—to a place where even the keenest mind cannot predict what comes next. These obedient leaders often take those entrusted to their care to a place where faith is more important than sense. However, someone has to execute that vision in the natural, and the successful execution relies largely on effectively conducted business. This is where faith intersects with the mechanics of getting the mission done.

The mechanics, or the "how," of carrying out your mission ought to be based on sound principles—not on a feeling or a hunch. Not on an opinion. Keep in mind that the church is not a business; the church merely conducts business. In everything the church does, we can bring glory to the King just as we do in a song, in a gathering, or in a soup kitchen. While winning souls or feeding the hungry are important, those tasks are just the tip of the spear; its shaft comprises the staffers, the donors, and the board members doing the work of the church in the natural. It is the tip of the spear that makes the spear a spear, but it's the shaft of the spear that makes the tip effective. Both parts need each other to be an effective tool in the hand of their heavenly Father.

Having spent decades conducting business for churches and ministries, I have seen leaders stretch the faith of the entire ministry many times by their God-led decisions that made little business sense. I've learned not to sweat it, but that wasn't always the case. Dealing with the "called ones" and respecting the different ways God works in their lives is often a challenge, but it's always an honor.

I once did some consulting work for a pastor whose ministry was facing a severe financial crisis. Bills were being paid late, and a payroll was coming up without any hope of being met. The bank accounts were almost depleted, and there was no expected income to count on. All they could do was wait until the tithes and offerings were collected the following Sunday. I had the unhappy job of telling the pastor how grim the situation looked.

When I stepped into his office, prepared with financial reports to prove the gravity of the situation, the pastor sat down at his desk, which was strewn with books and papers.

"I just don't know where the next dollar will come from," I told him bluntly. "We have bills we cannot pay. We need to think about shutting some things down."

He looked at me with watery eyes set in a tranquil face. "What is the value of a soul in heaven?" he asked me.

I had come armed with answers to any financial question he could have asked—except that one.

"I don't believe there is any way to measure that, sir," I told him.

The pastor responded, "I have spent over forty years being faithful to God's call on my life to win souls for His kingdom, and He has been faithful to provide the resources. If God has changed this plan, He has not told me; and until He does, I'm sticking to the plan. If, for some reason, God has decided He is done with me and this church—if this is my last day in ministry—I am going to be found faithful to the vision God gave me. God's ways are not our ways. Sometimes, we simply have to slip our hand into the Lord's and walk alongside Him in faith." Then he stood up from the desk. "I'm going now, and I'll be spending some time in prayer."

I noticed for the first time how disheveled his clothes were; and when I saw the blanket draped over the sofa against the wall, I realized that he'd already been in prayer, and I had interrupted him.

"Yes, sir!" I said.

His faith, juxtaposed against my lack of faith, made me ashamed. I realized then that while my role as a church business administrator was important, it was clear why God chose the "called ones," rather than businesspeople, to lead His church. I asked the Lord to forgive my doubt and to give me the courage and strength to stand in faith with this man who had such trust in Him.

This experience forever changed me. It was then that I submitted once and for all to God's call on my life to spend the rest of my days serving these choice servants of God.

It's true that businesspeople need to be among the voices heard at the table. But getting people to heaven, feeding the hungry, clothing the naked, visiting those who are in prison—these goals are always of utmost importance. God grants vision to the "called ones," and this is how He leads His church. Church staff, board members, consultants, and so forth—all those engaged in the business of ministry—have to adapt to this arrangement that Jesus has made for His church. If you don't believe in the leader of a church, then you shouldn't work there. If you don't believe in the vision of the church or charity, you should walk away quietly and do no harm. We must have enough faith to believe that when a leader is in the center of God's will, God will provide for the fulfillment of his vision.

Minding the Lord's business is a matter of stewardship. The church is not a business, but it *does* business. From lawyers to architects, computer programmers to Web developers, the church hires a host of professionals to carry out its goals in the natural. But when it comes to conducting business, many church leaders try to take care of things themselves, or to try to save money by hiring part-time or unqualified people—or, even worse, by delegating the job to volunteers. There are risks and costs, both seen and unseen, that arise when church business is left in the hands of the novice or underqualified. Yet these can be avoided rather than endured.

There is an ethic of business that should be followed. There are principles of business that are learned with time, training, and experience. In the end, it is the "called ones" whom God has appointed to lead His church, but they need the support of business leaders with enough faith to walk with these "crazy" people and say, "Yes, sir."

The story I just shared about the faith-filled pastor in dire financial straits has a God-sized ending. The pastor led the staff and elders in many prayer meetings. We trimmed the budget of every department, first getting rid of waste and maximizing efficiency. But we also spent every last penny on soul-winning outreach. We met one payroll and clung to our faith to meet the next. A month passed. When we had exhausted everything we could think of doing in the natural—when we'd come to the end of our own ideas, when there was nothing left but faith—someone walked into the church office in the middle of the week and handed the church secretary an envelope. In it was the largest financial gift ever given to the church, and it covered all the loose ends.

Since then, I'll admit that when I have difficulty balancing a church's budget, I find myself asking the church secretary if something—anything—was left on her desk. It doesn't often happen that way, of course. But the value of faith cannot be overstated, even as businesspeople seek to operate Christian churches and ministries according to business principles that glorify God while also following whatever instructions God has spoken to the "called ones."

In the chapters that follow, I'd like to share some key business principles to employ in the church in order to move the mission forward and glorify God in the process.

PART I:

MANAGEMENT

CHAPTER 1

"PRICE" IS NOT THE SAME AS "COST"

When your utmost desire is to win people to Christ, then the primary cost to concern yourself with should be the people who aren't won because of the things you choose not to do. In conducting Christian business, we need to keep in mind that we are talking about a really big God who says the stars and planets are but vapor in His breath. That's pretty big. The church incurs a cost because of what we fail to do for Him—a concept whose equivalent in the business realm is known as "opportunity cost," or the price of either not doing a thing or doing nothing. This is the true cost of the western church in the last fifty years.

I was trying to help a certain pastor friend who was struggling with the question most churches have grappled with over the past three decades: Shall we change? This particular pastor wanted to shed the ministerial robe he traditionally donned on Sunday mornings, disband the choir, and stop using hymnals. He met with his team, all of whom were in favor of the proposed changes. They wanted to meet the needs of their contemporary neighborhood with contemporary means.

They talked about the changes endlessly, and even leaked the ideas to the parishioners. Many of them were thrilled at the prospect, while others grumbled. The pastor assured the grumblers that the changes wouldn't be forced on them but would rather be optional. This assurance settled them down. Meanwhile, the staff continued to discuss the myriad ways to effect a transition to a more contemporary service. A year went by, but no date was set for making the switch. No one could reach a decision.

The staff's lack of decisiveness had nothing to do with the will of God. They were all in agreement that God wanted them to change. Their indecision came right down to not wanting to deal with those whose feathers would be ruffled by the changes. They kept telling themselves they were easing into the change to be wise, but they weren't wise at all. Would Jesus have entered their staff meeting and said, "Please don't change things. This church has been shrinking for years. Keep it up"?

The biggest cost to most churches is "opportunity cost." There is no immediate physical cost for doing nothing. But the ongoing cost that's accrued by doing nothing is that no new people come to church, no new families are saved, fewer and fewer orphans are cared for, and so forth. When we talk something to death yet do nothing to act on it, we're accruing "opportunity cost."

Let's say a church missions committee plans a fund-raiser banquet, and in selecting the menu, someone has the bright idea not to offend the vegetarians. Now, I'm not bashing vegetarians. But this type of reasoning easily becomes a slippery slope that leads to distraction from the primary purpose—in this case, to raise funds. The committee's goal becomes not to offend people with diabetes, high blood pressure, or diverticulitis. They carefully look at every dollar spent, and yet they freely spend time and resources on all the wrong stuff. Because they spend so much time and effort planning a menu that caters to a select few instead of focusing on how they could raise the most money, their net profits are lower than they otherwise would have been. And the money they didn't raise because they were focused on superficial things—that's "opportunity cost." It's potential income that was sacrificed unnecessarily.

When you consider potential projects, you ask, "What is the cost of this?" and "What is the cost of that?" But what you're really asking for are prices. In business terms, the difference between price and cost is explained this way: Price is what you pay for a thing, and cost is what you give up, don't get, or give away.

It's like investing. You always measure the value of an investment by the return it produces for you. Price is what you pay; return is what you get. In the church, the most important return is the number of people we reach for Christ; the cost is a measure of the resources we allocate toward reaching people for Christ, plus the number of people we fail to reach (opportunity cost) because of our indecisiveness, ineffectiveness, and so forth.

Simply put, "opportunity costs" are the things that do not happen because of a course of action not taken. In the past forty years, the Western church has gone from being a leading force in a Christian culture to a religious sect in a secular culture. How did that happen?

Recently, while trying to help a local church raise funds for its building campaign, I was turned down for a loan at the bank. This church had been a beacon in the community for over a hundred years and a customer of the bank for almost four decades. When I asked the banker to explain his refusal, he said, "While the bank appreciates our long business relationship with the church, the loan committee views churches as depreciating assets in a declining industry, and the committee members have no appetite for lending to an organization in that environment."

What the banker was saying is, "When we look at the church, we see nothing happening." There was a time when banks fought to do business with the local church because of the resulting boost in the bank's reputation. Do you think the church has come to this point for all it has *done* over the last forty years or for what it has *not* done?

What about your church? Do you spend more time talking about what people inside the church like or don't like—or what the people outside the church need? Do you expend more energy trying to avoid conflict or trying to change lives? Do you spend more time talking or doing? Every choice has a cost, and every cost has a corresponding return. On which does your church focus? "Return on investment" in the church is best measured by the number of lives changed. Cost should be measured by how many people won't hear the gospel and whose lives will never change because of the things we in the church choose not to do.

Here is a little exercise for you to try. Think of all the people you know of who gave their heart to Jesus at your church in the last year. Now, double that number to account for the people who gave their heart to Jesus without making it public knowledge. Next, divide your church's annual budget by that number. You now have a value that represents the dollar amount that your church spends for each new soul it sends to heaven. Are you proud of that amount?

Here is the really meaningful part of this exercise. If you wanted to cut the "cost per soul sent to heaven" at your church in half, would it be easier to double the number of salvations or to cut your budget in half? Now, take five minutes and write down every idea you can think of that could increase the number of salvations in your church in the next twelve months. For example, you could include an altar call at the end of each service, or you could invite a soul-winning evangelist to hold a revival at your church. Whatever ideas you generate, the souls that don't go to heaven next year, and the lives not changed—these represent the opportunity cost of not pursuing the ideas you just wrote down.

If you are a church leader, you should get this concept of opportunity cost into your own spirit, as well as into the spirit of the people you lead. Then, direct your budget accordingly. Call me in a year, and we will celebrate together how God honored your decision.

You cannot measure costs simply in terms of dollars, resources, and time. Start viewing the money your church spends as an investment in heaven, not an amount spent on goods and services. And then, most important, measure costs in people not going to heaven and the amount of people who won't hear the gospel if you do the safe, easy thing instead of the "scary," God thing.

⌇

Minding His Business Basic Principle:

The greatest cost most churches will incur is "opportunity cost"—the price of doing the safe, easy thing—or, even worse, doing nothing—instead of the "scary" God thing.

CHAPTER 2

NOTHING MOVES WITHOUT FRICTION

A pastor and I walked out of church together after a wonderful Sunday morning service that had been capped off by a "pastor's coffee" for new members. The church property had once seemed enormous for the tiny congregation the pastor led. They had started by building a small classroom complex and kept adding on. Now, the cavernous sanctuary was surrounded by newly paved parking lots to accommodate the exploding membership.

I had been called in to help fine-tune some growth strategies, nothing more. But as I surveyed the property, I couldn't help noticing a major problem on a weed-covered corner of the lot, just beyond the last area that had been paved. The dilapidated shell of a small wooden building was still standing there, abandoned long before the congregation had purchased the parcel of land. The overgrowth had finally reached the edge of the property, posing just as big a hazard as the old, run-down building.

The pastor and I stood on the top step just outside the front doors of the church, breathing in the beautiful autumn air and basking in the sense of satisfaction that comes after a successful service. It is not unusual for me to ruin such moments, and this day was no different. I was ethically compelled to bring up the problem I'd identified.

"Wonderful day!" I said. "But let me show you something. Look how close your parking lot is to that abandoned building."

The pastor looked straight at the building. He knew without my needing to indicate what I was talking about.

"It really concerns me," I said. "While you were speaking with the new members, I saw some children playing in and around that building as they waited for their parents. I'm sorry to tell you that it looks like an accident or a lawsuit just waiting to happen."

"I've meant to tear that down for a long time," the pastor said. "With so much going on, I just haven't given it much thought."

"We can get a local construction company to tear it down and haul it away," I told him.

"How much will it cost?" he wanted to know.

"I have no idea," I said. "I've never had to destroy a building before. I'll get some bids, and we'll find out."

"Don't bother getting bids," the pastor said. "Larry Green is a contractor in our church. He'll do a great job. I'll call him tomorrow."

I was handed Larry's proposal the following week. I didn't know the first thing about tearing down a building and hauling it away, but I had predicted the cost would be in the thousands of dollars. Instead, the bid was in the high five figures. Just looking at the number made me feel uneasy. All I could think of were all those new members, and that the outreach budget would need to be slashed just because of an old building that needed to be properly disposed of.

I took the proposal into the pastor's office. "We can't spend this much just to clear away that building," I told him.

"Well, we can't offend Larry, now that we've asked him to give us a price," the pastor countered. "I'm sure he's done his best."

This was not a happy moment, but all forward movement causes friction. What I had to do was get the facts—to gather bids from other local contractors. Then, I asked for a special meeting with the pastor to lay out those facts. All the other bids were cheaper than Larry's by far. The pastor saw the problem. Now, he would have to talk to Larry and let him know that his bid was rejected—an unpleasant prospect. We can tell ourselves that, as Christians, we should always want what is best for the church. But "should" is no guarantee of what actually is.

When we are faced with unpleasant circumstances, such as a difficult conversation, we have to remember that wherever there is movement, there is going to be friction. Even an airplane flying has a coefficient of airflow that creates lift. If there's no friction, nothing is moving. Churches are known for easing the friction in people's lives, by smoothing the aftermath of suffering caused by sin. But whenever the church makes progress in its mission, there is going to be friction; otherwise, there won't be forward movement.

Think of the game of football. Every time I played as a kid, I came home bruised. Being banged up at least a little was part of the game. No one was too concerned about the bruises, either. My parents, the schoolteachers, the rest of the guys—we all knew that some scrapes and scars were part and parcel of playing the game we loved.

As it turned out, Larry handled the situation well. He told the pastor that his company wasn't equipped to handle a small job like that efficiently, anyway. Instead of balking at being passed over for the task, he asked to see the other bids. He warned the pastor about one of the companies that he knew not to be reputable, and the pastor ended up asking Larry to select the company to use. The job was done properly, and at a fraction of the cost we would have incurred by hiring Larry.

In ministry, as we make progress in doing what we love—seeing people come to Christ—we are bound to get a bit banged up. We create friction. It's not just *part* of advancing the ministry; it's *essential* to advancing the ministry. The church, especially in the western hemisphere, has been bending over backward so as not to offend anyone for the last forty years. And where has it gotten us? Avoiding conflict is a luxury no church or ministry can afford.

Again, nothing moves without friction. A responsible businessperson in the church doesn't worry about the anxiety he might create by bringing a problem to the attention of a church leader. Church business leaders owe it to their spiritual leaders to speak the truth, regardless of the inevitable friction. It's like football: Even if you love the sport, you can expect to come home a little bruised after every game.

◡⁀

Minding His Business **Basic Principle:**

There is always friction when there is movement. Don't fear it. You can't have one without the other.

CHAPTER 3

THE ETHIC OF BUSINESS

It's not personal, it's business." In many movies, that line is spoken just before someone gets murdered, fired, or dumped on in some way—usually, an act that springs from motives that are, in fact, quite personal.

But in real life, business really *must* be just business. Business isn't personal unless someone makes something personal out of a business activity or decision. Decisions have to be made. One idea has to be chosen among all the options. One vendor will always outbid the others. One employee will always do a better job than the rest. These are the business realities of life, and they apply to kingdom work, as well.

One day, a friend called me to ask a favor. He wanted me to talk to a friend of his who pastored an older church in a rough part of town. For five years, young people had been streaming into the area and taking over. Run-down convenience stores, upholsterers, barber shops, and shoe repair stores were being replaced by gourmet taco stands, bagel bakeries, and trendy novelty shops that were attracting a new clientele.

After looking over the demographics of the area around the church, I called the pastor. He was excited right from the start of the conversation.

"For twenty-five years, this area has been in decline," the pastor said. "We've shrunk along with it and were able to keep going only because we had the property paid for. But now, all of a sudden, we cannot open our doors without new visitors streaming in. People are even dropping by in the middle of the week to shake my hand and ask about our beliefs. They're not even put off by my age. They're young and just seeking a way to find the Lord. It's wonderful."

I thought he was going to burst into tears. His genuine desire to reach the newcomers in his community touched my heart. This was someone I felt I could really help. It would be a challenge, but it was exciting.

At our first face-to-face meeting, I learned that the pastor's support staff consisted of a part time associate pastor, a director of children's ministries, a facilities manager, and a volunteer worship leader. Those positions were all they really needed for the size of the congregation at that time. One of the first things I talked to him about was the need for a church Web site. We discussed a few potential strategies, and I made an appointment to meet with his staff members.

By the time of the next meeting, the pastor had already talked to the staff about constructing a Web site. They had all agreed that they needed one. I had pulled some strings for them and found a way to develop what they needed, complete with a strategy to make members out of visitors, all for just a few thousand dollars. I laid the plan out for them, but as soon as I mentioned the cost, they pulled back.

"I have a friend whose brother is a really talented Web designer," the associate pastor said. "I already talked to him.

He and his friend can build what we need for only five hundred dollars."

Several others made suggestions of their own before I brought the conversation back around to my original idea. I explained that maintaining a professional Web site would require more than a couple of guys doing it in their free time, regardless of how talented they might be. That led to another round of discussions.

Although the staff still wasn't sold on the idea, I went ahead and showed them a visual conceptualization of the Web design. This led to even more discussion. Everyone on the team seemed to lose sight of the purpose behind the Web site as they advanced their personal opinions on how it ought to look.

"I'd like for the team to get in agreement on this," the pastor said. "If we can't be unanimous, then maybe we should think about it some more."

We scheduled another meeting, at which the staff rehashed the same pros and cons that had been established at the previous meeting. And the associate pastor recommended the exact same Web designer he'd suggested in the first meeting.

"I think I've done all that I can do," I told my friend over the phone later that week.

"So fast?" he asked. "Is the church going to grow?"

"That's going to be up to them," I told him. "The pastor doesn't want to be the 'bad guy' and make a decision that might be unpopular with his staff. He's listening to people who don't know what they're talking about, as well as listening to me, the business guy."

My friend went to bat behind the scenes and explained to his pastor buddy that he should heed the voice of experience rather than continue giving ear to the opinions of his staff, none of whom had experience in Web design or building a business. But the pastor never contacted me again. My friend kept me abreast of their progress. Two years after my second meeting with the staff, the church still didn't have a Web site in place. Meanwhile, a church just three blocks down the street had a fantastic Web site—and a youthful congregation that was growing steadily.

The pastor had taken what should have been a business decision, turned it into a personal decision, and thereby put a stop to any forward progress. Please don't make the same mistake.

~

Minding His Business **Basic Principle:**

Turning business decisions into matters of personal preference causes progress to grind to a halt. It is better to reach many outside your church and risk upsetting a few inside your church than to reach only a few and upset no one.

CHAPTER 4

EMBRACE CONFLICT AS A SIGN OF GROWTH

Christian leaders are called, in essence, to help laypeople to resolve personal problems and interpersonal conflicts by the power of Christ. As a result, most people view conflict as something bad that ought to be avoided at all costs.

The growth of a church or ministry will inevitably give way to some conflict. Growth always prompts anxiety among certain people. The only way to avoid any conflict is to do nothing—to stagnate in a state of complacent inertia. In conducting the business of ministry, we cannot shirk from conflict just because it may prove unpleasant. If we do, we will miss the greater, positive outcome. In the process of growth, there is almost always going to be conflict—and there is *always* going to be a price to pay for avoiding conflict at all costs.

In minding His business, it always comes back to stewardship. We have to ask ourselves, are we going to cut programs and/or spend extra money on superficial things in order to avoid hurting someone's feelings? Or are we going to be good stewards of our resources?

Again, the cost of avoiding conflict is often high. Here's an example.

In a well-known ministry, a famed worship leader led the music with flourish at each conference. He had long since stopped selling records, writing best-selling songs, and touring on his own. For the better part of two decades, he'd traveled exclusively with this ministry. He was an institution. He was also the highest-paid employee on the books.

I was called in by the board of this ministry because, in spite of their long sequence of great "glory years," their tremendous service to the Christian community, and their high-profile reputation, they were shrinking. They asked me to help them develop a new marketing strategy geared toward attracting new members. I was eager to work with them, not least of all because I owned several albums of their worship leader's recordings and looked forward to the prospect of meeting him.

At my first session with the ministry's executive team, I was surprised that the worship leader was in attendance. I was even more surprised by his cantankerous demeanor. Now, I'm never surprised when people treat me rudely after I suggest reducing their paycheck or downsizing their job. But this individual was downright rude just because I existed. I left that meeting wondering about his spiritual state rather than feeling grateful to have finally met him.

As I looked over the facts and figures the team had given me, I was astonished to see that attendance at their conferences had shrunk by 70 percent over the past decade. Seventy percent! No wonder they'd called me in. The message they shared was tremendous, and their ministry was still relevant. There was no reason why they shouldn't have still been a powerhouse for God. What happened? I carefully reviewed the records of ticket purchases and discovered that very few people attended one of their conferences a second time in the same city.

I started interviewing staff members and called a few select donors. During each of these conversations, without my prompting, the person I was speaking with mentioned that it was difficult for the ministry to get the same local volunteer musicians and singers to agree to participate a second time, and that the worship leader was disrespectful of the very donors whose financial contributions covered his salary. I myself had observed that the entire staff tiptoed around him, trying to keep him happy. After all, he was a famous worship leader. He had written songs sung all over the country. He was a star.

I brought the executives together and told them their rate of attrition. I asked for their help in brainstorming ways to reverse the negative trend.

"Let's do a survey," the marketing director suggested, "to find out what people really want."

"Great idea!" the president said. "We could ask the people who come what makes them want to return."

"I agree that a survey might be helpful," I said, "but I want to survey the people who came one year and *didn't* come back the next." I knew of a fairly inexpensive way to pull this off, and by the end of the meeting, the executive staff was in agreement.

When I tabulated the survey results, I presented them to the ministry president. It had been his belief that nothing needed to change; they had only to get more newcomers in the doors, and they would rock along for years to come. Understandably, he was stunned by the survey results and what they revealed. A full 91 percent of the respondents who attended the conference only once identified the quality of the music as one of the top three things they disliked. A staggering 33 percent of the respondents said the quality of music was their number one reason for deciding not to return the following year.

The president was hesitant to confront the worship leader. For years, he had chosen to endure the man's rude manners and erratic ways rather than search for a replacement, not wanting to deal with the conflict that would result from ruffling the feathers of the music leader—especially conflict with staff members and donors who felt that the artist was indispensable to the ministry.

What the president did not realize was the high price he was paying for avoiding that conflict. As he'd put up with the worship leader's insolence, for fear of the fallout of replacing him, 70 percent of his audience had walked away.

I can't tell you the number of times I've had to sit down with a church leader or ministry staffer and say, "I'm sorry, but we have to move forward. The problem is, we can't get where we need to go without creating a conflict with you. It breaks my heart to say that."

Delaying decisions and deliberately ignoring problems has become almost an art form in the church today. We measure success as inversely proportionate to the number of people we upset, thereby making "Do nothing" the number one choice of strategy in the church. Not far behind "Do nothing" as a strategy choice is "Talk about it later," with the result of indefinite postponement.

The church needs to learn to measure success in terms of the number of people who are reached and who return. If we embrace conflict when it signals growth and expansion, we can address the conflict and keep growing. But if we avoid conflict at all costs, we end up trapping ourselves in a state of stagnation.

〜

Minding His Business **Basic Principle:**

Achieving greater positives usually requires enduring lesser negatives. Get the greater positive by addressing the lesser negative.

CHAPTER 5

WISDOM COSTS, BUT EXPERIENCE IS EXPENSIVE

In the book of Proverbs, we read that wisdom yields better returns than gold (see Proverbs 3:13–14), and that we should "buy" wisdom, even if it costs everything we have (see Proverbs 4:7).

The reason for hiring people with "experience" is because they actually have had "experiences." If those people had only victories, they wouldn't have wisdom. But if they have had failures and losses, then they have the wisdom which is the benefit of those experiences.

Again, experience is what you learn from your own mistakes; wisdom is what you learn from the mistakes of others. (The latter is, of course, a less painful way of learning a lesson.) Most churches and ministries gain experience from making unwise decisions and suffering as a result. That's why experience is never gained without pain. Wisdom will cost you, too; but a lack of wisdom costs more, because, if you don't have wisdom, you usually experience pain.

Wisdom is what we need *before* we make a choice. Experience is what we gain *after* we have made our choice. Your goal should be to always learn from the mistakes of others, so that you may be equipped to make good, sound decisions instead of having to suffer the painful experience of a poor choice.

The reason that experienced businesspeople don't suffer fools well is that they've suffered so many fools. They're skeptical because their experiences have taught them to be slow to trust, lest they suffer betrayal. After all, in order to be stabbed in the back, you have to give someone your back. Prudent businesspeople are analytical because their experience has taught them that it is smart to keep their personal feelings from clouding their judgment.

Whenever I meet a young pastor, the first thing I tell him is, "Go find an old pastor." Young pastors need to be mentored by spiritual fathers whose experiences will give them the wisdom to to share with the young pastor.

The next thing I tell every young pastor is this: "Find a mature businessperson and take him to lunch once a month so you can run your ideas past someone who is wise in the ways of business." The odds are pretty good that the perspective of a seasoned businessperson and that of a young pastor are going to diverge in most cases. The young pastor can learn from considering the perspective of the old businessperson. And he should.

The story I'm about to tell recounts one of the most painful things I've ever had to watch, so consider yourself warned. The problem stemmed from a failure to place adequate value on experience or to spend enough time seeking wisdom.

A young pastor and his wife started a church by knocking on doors in their neighborhood. The couple launched the church with services held in the auditorium of a local high school. Over time, they generated a following of faithful members who were generous givers. The auditorium started to fill, and they soon decided they needed a permanent building of their own. That's when they brought me in, to run a capital fund-raising drive.

One of the first questions I asked was, "Have you talked to any banks yet?"

The young pastor said, "Why do I need to talk to a bank for a capital fund-raising drive?"

"Well, do you expect to raise four million dollars from your six hundred people?"

"No, we'll need a loan."

"Banks don't have an appetite to loan money to churches that have met for only a few years in a rented space," I explained. "Potential lenders don't see a church with the faith of a young pastor. Potential lenders look at churches as depreciating assets in a declining industry."

I tried to convince this young pastor to talk to at least several banks before he asked his congregation to give sacrificially. It would be much wiser to ask a congregation to give money toward a plan that had been approved by a lender than to ask a lender for the money to cover a vision shared by six hundred people.

We discussed some fund-raising strategies, but it wasn't long before I had to walk away. This young pastor was so sure of himself, and so stubborn in his ignorance, that he couldn't hear me.

The pastor moved forward with the capital campaign, asking the members of his church to give sacrificially. In all, the congregation pledged a million dollars. But when the pastor approached several different banks in their city to ask for the remaining funds, he was turned down. No one would loan money to an independent church with no denominational or regional oversight. Not to mention, the pastor himself had bad credit. The building project never got off the ground.

When his parishioners started asking him, "What about my five grand that I gave sacrificially?" the pastor called me back, asking for advice. I suggested he tell the people the truth: that it would take another couple of years to raise enough money to fund the building project. I told him they would all grow together through the process, and he would learn something from God.

But, once again, he didn't listen. When someone donated a prime piece of property, and a contractor from the congregation stepped up, the decision was made to handle the building project themselves. Church members came out to the site on weekends to help with the construction, excited to watch it go up. But then, as winter set in, people's enthusiasm began to wane; and the building was nowhere near done. And then, sure enough, they ran out of cash. People lost confidence and started leaving the church.

The halfway-completed building sat there, unused, for a few years. A wise man would have considered selling the land to generate enough money to keep the congregation growing, but the pastor didn't do that. The church membership disintegrated, and the pastor moved to a different community, where he secured a secular job. The few parishioners who'd remained on the board sold the property in order to pay the remaining bills before closing the church down for good.

Of course, there were a lot of meetings and conversations and drama that occurred during this period of decline. The end result was that someone finally bought the land and razed the incomplete structure built by the million dollars of a congregation long since disbanded.

Allow this pitiful story to underscore the point that bringing in someone with wisdom, and listening to him, is far less painful— and costs far less—than having the experience yourself.

~

Minding His Business Basic Principle:

Get wisdom. In the long run, wisdom is less expensive and far less painful than experience.

MANAGEMENT

CHAPTER 6

ACCOUNTABILITY IS A JOB

A pastor was fed up with hearing people complain about the temperature in the sanctuary. One Sunday morning, he stood before the congregation and asked for a show of hands from those who felt it was too warm. A bunch of hands shot up. Then he asked for a show of hands from those who felt it was too cold. More hands shot up. Then he said, "Please trade places with each other, so that I can preach."

In any organization, whether it's a church or a secular business, the truth is that if you turn left, certain people are going to be mad; if you turn right, a different group of people are going to be mad. Don't be deceived: The success of an endeavor does not correlate with the number of people who get ticked off.

In any organization, action and accountability create the traction that causes things to move forward. Everything that moves requires energy and traction, and, as we've discussed, nothing moves without creating friction.

Traditional wisdom tells churches to attract more people by increasing their parking and polishing the nursery. But if you really want to be effective, it's more important to increase your *accountability* and polish your *character*.

Accountability is probably practiced by about 50 percent of the population. Some people do what they say they are going to do, and some people don't. Guess which group doesn't value accountability and tends to initiate conflict when held to it?

Most church leaders are creative, relational people—visionaries who see the big picture and the tiny details all at once. And most creative, relational people don't like conflict. There's nothing wrong with being the person who God made you to be, unless you operate your organization according to the ethos that says, "We upset someone, so our efforts failed." When leaders equate ruffled feathers with failure, they start avoiding conflict at all costs—and they sacrifice forward progress, as a result. Remember, upsetting no one—eliminating friction—comes at the expense of growth and forward movement.

One church for which I did some consulting had been started by a pastor who was a real creative, relational person. He hired a children's minister and a music director. So, there were three creative, relational people working together. They would get together and talk endlessly about big ideas they never followed through with. No one held them accountable for it, either. The net result was a ton of talk and only an ounce of results. It's hard to get anything meaningful done or to achieve any growth in an environment like that.

Another church I worked with hosted a huge event every summer that drew thousands of people. Many of the church's members had started attending regularly after coming to this event. But there were so many moving parts to this gathering that it was always difficult to pull off. Every summer, when the event ended, at least one manager or director would quit. This became so commonplace that the staff began placing bets on who would be the one to quit each summer.

When the church fell on tough economic times, they asked me to help them balance the budget to avoid having to cancel the annual event. Upon investigating the situation, I discovered that surprisingly few people had attended the event the previous summer, with a resulting loss of a significant amount of money. When it got down to it, they really called me only because they were on the verge of bankruptcy, and they thought I might be able to pull them out.

In my first meeting with the staff, which was held six months before the event was scheduled to take place, I saw that all the leaders had come armed with a pen and a legal pad of blank pages. They all contributed to the conversation, most of them taking notes as they did so. At our second meeting, five months prior to the event, the staff all showed up with legal pads again—and the pages were blank. In the month that had passed since the previous meeting, nothing had happened. I started conducting individual interviews and quickly learned that this pattern repeated itself every year. It would get worse and worse as the event drew closer, until someone was finally driven to quit.

I restructured the budget and adjusted the timeline, got the buy-in of most of the leaders, and then started holding weekly meetings. At our first weekly session, I asked a secretary to record the specific action items we discussed—in other words, who does what by when. (A plan is really just a series of action items with a corresponding budget.)

After our first meeting, I took the list of action items and e-mailed each person a reminder of what he was responsible for doing, adding that he would be expected to report on his progress at the meeting the following week.

At the second meeting, we went around the room and gave each leader a chance to share about the progress he had made on his action item. It turned out that very few had even read the e-mail I had sent.

By the third meeting, some of the leaders were getting uncomfortable. They had failed to do what they had said they would do, and they were beginning to realize that I wasn't about to relent in my expectation that they follow through. And the more the responsible leaders shared how they had accomplished their action items, the harsher the spotlight shone on those who had done nothing.

By the fourth week, almost every leader was able to report that he had achieved his action item. Now, we could finally get somewhere. The previous year, the church had paid tens of thousands of dollars on extra last-minute "rush" projects. Now, we were coming in under budget because the staff had allowed themselves enough time to trim even the projected costs without rush fees to worry about.

The event went off with only a few token bumps and scratches. The church generated enough of a profit that they were able to pay off some of the debt they'd incurred the previous summer. To this day, they still host the event every summer. They had the ability to pull it off and earn a profit all along; they just needed some accountability.

One of the most neglected parts of management, especially in churches, is accountability. And the most neglected part of accountability is consequences. The lack of both is slowly killing the church. Direction without accountability is like a race with no start. Accountability without consequences is like a race with no finish line. Without a start, there is no race. Without a finish line, there are no results.

If you and your staff have been talking about the same big ideas for a long time, and you are tired of just talking about the vision God gave you, start asking the question, "Who will do what, and by when?" Then, make a list of action items, who is responsible for accomplishing each one, and the consequences of a failure to do so. Some will engage. Some will adapt. Some will resist. Some will rebel. Reward those who engage. Praise those who adapt. Demote those (from leadership) who resist. Discipline those who rebel.

∼

Minding His Business Basic Principle:

Assigning and reviewing action items is the foundation of accountability. "Who is supposed to do what, and by when?" is a question that all excellent leaders ask, and all excellent staff members answer, on a daily basis.

CHAPTER 7

THE SEVEN CARDINAL RULES OF STAFF MEETINGS

Apastor friend kept bragging to me about how effective his team was. As we discussed the team members, it became apparent that he had great affection for each of them. When I asked if he had any critiques or concerns whatsoever, he thought for a moment, then said, "We spend a great deal of time in meetings talking, but we don't seem to turn a lot of that talk into results."

I asked him to tell me more about these meetings. He suggested I come spend a day with his team and then offer suggestions on how to improve their effectiveness.

I accepted his invitation and attended their next staff meeting. It was a blast!

The agenda could be summarized like this: Talk about the previous Sunday's service, get teary-eyed about one parishioner's situation, laugh at three funny stories, broadly discuss what they could do better next Sunday, mention the far-off Easter season (this was the end of January, so it wasn't really that far off), and conclude with lunch. Lots of talk, lots of love, lots of ideas, and lots of opinions—but nothing in the meeting seemed designed to translate talk into action.

As it turned out, the pastor was absolutely right—he had a great team of people who loved Jesus, loved the church, loved the pastor, and loved one another. So it came as a shock to him when I asked to see the church's financial reports and membership records. I felt I had to, since he'd asked me for help. As I suspected, the church hadn't grown in several years, by any measurement. Why? Because they gauged their success by how much they enjoyed their work and how much affection they had for one another, not by how effective their work was or any measurable criteria.

I decided to share with the pastor what I call the "Seven Cardinal Rules for Staff Meetings":

1. *Staff meetings must occur at the same time on the same day every week.* The first meeting you reschedule to accommodate a specific person sets a dangerous precedent. Your staffers will come up with excuse after excuse, believing themselves to be the exception to the rule. Trying to find a time that works for everyone to assemble on a weekly basis is a waste of energy. Set a day and a time, and stick to it.

2. *Staff meetings have only two purposes: to provide information and to keep people accountable.* Providing information helps avoid train wrecks. The information that is discussed should not come as a surprise to anyone; but if it does catch someone unawares, it just means you avoided a train wreck that would have happened had you not met.

Assigning and managing action items are the foundation of any system of accountability, and yet assigning action items is probably one of the most neglected necessities of any church staff. At every staff meeting, the action items established at the previous meeting ought to be reviewed, and a new list of assignments should be made. Without the inclusion of action items, meetings drag on with little productivity to show for their length, which is the primary reason many people come to dread them.

3. *Staff meetings must be brief.* Most people are able to devote their focus to any given thing for forty minutes, on average. That means that a staff meeting lasting 45 minutes to an hour is a long meeting for most attention spans. The ideal meeting length, in my opinion, is thirty minutes.

In one church where I couldn't get the staff on track, I took all the chairs out of the conference room. The first stand-up meeting was far shorter than any previous one. The second was shorter still. When we established a pattern of brief yet productive meetings, I had the chairs brought in again.

4. *Staff meetings are not for solving problems.* Decisions, solutions, and plans are to be developed outside the staff meetings by the designated people. At a staff meeting, the presiding officer may bring up an issue for several minutes' worth of discussion, but then he should say, "Please meet/research/consult/solve over this coming week and report back your decision at our next meeting."

5. *Staff meetings should include only as many people as absolutely need to be present.* There shouldn't be too many people in the room. When you talk about topics that are not relevant to everyone, or on which not everyone has expertise, it alienates a portion of the participants, who stay quiet and contribute nothing. And when you broach a topic that's too trite or too popular, suddenly everyone's an expert; all voices compete to be heard, creating unnecessary friction. I'll give you an example.

In a recent church staff meeting, the pastor included the entire staff—twelve people in all. The leadership team—consisting of four people—brainstormed a strategy for converting visitors into members. They went down the list, discussing everything from branding to marketing communication. Meanwhile, the eight other people in the room sat there mutely because they had no knowledge of such subjects.

One part of the six-figure plan was to create a café where the congregants could gather following a service. When the conversation drifted toward the menu—what kinds of cookies they should sell on Sundays, and for how much—everyone came to life; for who doesn't know something about cookies?

"The grocery store cookies are better than the food supplier cookies, for the same price!" someone said. "We can't charge people for cookies that we used to give away free!" someone else put in. "We can't give free coffee and charge for cookies!" "If we give free coffee and cookies, we're going to lose our shirts!" "We could have volunteers bake cookies...." "Have you ever tasted Sister Sarah's cookies? Her white chocolate walnut cookies are to die for!"

After ticking through the agenda in thirty minutes flat, the officer presiding over the meeting lost all control, as the "cookies and coffee" conversation went on for an hour. (I am not making this up.)

6. *At staff meetings, your silence is your approval.* This is an extraordinarily important ethos for any leadership team to keep in mind. People cannot *not* communicate. Eighty percent of communication is nonverbal. But silence requires interpretation. As such, it is important that a team agree ahead of time on how to interpret it. I strongly recommend that you establish with your team that silence indicates agreement. If someone doesn't speak up at a staff meeting, it can safely be assumed that he is 100 percent on board with the decisions that are announced. And in the case that someone is unhappy about a decision, he ought to schedule a meeting with the person responsible for the corresponding action item in order to discuss it.

Operating as a democracy is fair; but can you think of any high-functioning, highly productive, and extremely effective democracy? If you insist on everyone being in agreement with every decision or course of action, you will probably end up accomplishing nothing.

7. *All electronic devices must be turned off.* Whenever I attend a working lunch, I ask that all electronic devices be placed in the center of the table; the first person to reach for his smartphone or iPad gets to pay the bill. There is no excuse for an electronic device to interrupt a smooth-flowing meeting. If someone is awaiting an urgent word on the outcome of a loved one's surgical procedure, the birth of a baby, or a banker's decision, he should leave his phone with a trusted staffer who will interrupt the meeting, if need be.

Staff meetings are necessary. Do them, do them well, and move your mission forward.

∽

Minding His Business Basic Principle:

Staff meetings should be brief and should serve only for sharing information and assigning action items, not for making decisions.

CHAPTER 8

KICKING THE CAN DOWN THE ROAD

Famed eighteenth-century poet and thinker Samuel Johnson wrote, "Such...is the state of life, that none are happy but by the anticipation of change; the change itself is nothing; when we have made it the next wish is to change again."

In church life, however, the opposite is true: Few, if any, are happy at the anticipation of change. Making a change is often the most difficult feat facing a leader, a staff member, or a congregation.

A few years ago, I was called in to help a traditional urban church. In its heyday, they had boasted an attendance of one thousand. For thirty years, they had been known for having one of the best sacred choirs in the state, and they performed in one of the most beautiful cathedrals. But for the last ten years, the church had been experiencing a steady decline.

The neighborhood was changing. There had been an influx of young people of a different race from that of the congregants who had worshipped in the church on that corner for over a hundred years. The church's style of worship was dated and growing less popular by the year. In order to reach the demographic of the surrounding neighborhood, the church needed to contemporize the style of its praise and worship, among other things. But the choir director insisted that no changes be made. He said, "If God wanted church music to be popular, He would make sacred music popular."

Many of the faithful tithers and longtime members of the church sang in the choir and loved the director. If the pastor demanded that the choir director change the music style, "people were going to be unhappy." "People would leave." "The church would shrink."

The leadership was fully aware of the problem. Everyone stood by and talked about the church and its shrinking finances. No one made a decision for years. This is what I call "kicking the can down the road." No one stops to pick it up. No one attempts to remove the problem. No one tries to fix what's wrong. Instead, everybody simply kicks it forward for somebody else to deal with someday.

The pastor was nearing retirement and he didn't want to spend his final years making hard decisions, so he opted to leave them for the next pastor to address. By the time a new pastor was installed, attendance was down to 450 on Sundays. The congregation was aging rapidly. The new pastor left, and the whole church chose to kick the can down the road again.

Today, the congregation numbers 200, and the choir is mediocre. The very thing they wanted to avoid has happened. People left. The church shrank.

Another church had developed two worship services, one traditional and one contemporary, averaging an attendance of 500 and 200, respectively. Some people recommended swapping the times of the services, so that the contemporary service would be held later in the day rather than at 8 a.m.; but the leadership wanted to be cautious and keep their longtime members happy, so they opted to keep the traditional worship service at the more popular 10 a.m. time slot. Attendance at the contemporary service was growing, but the traditional service still drew a larger group and generated a greater amount of financial gifts. The leadership decided to kick the can down the road rather than move the growing service to a more convenient, more popular hour.

By the time I was called in to help, I found that 75 percent of first-time visitors had attended the 10 a.m. service. After that, even if they came back as many as three times, 80 percent eventually quit attending. Why? New people were not bound by sentiment or tradition and were more comfortable with a contemporary form of worship, but the time of that service was viewed as an inconvenience.

Everyone knew what needed to be done, but no one wanted to make the hard decision to flip the time slots or to add a new one. Even when presented with the numbers, the church leadership still refused to change the times of their services. They kicked the can down the road rather than risk upsetting a portion of the 500 people attending the traditional service.

Over time, what we saw was that the cost of refusing to change was not the 200-person decline in the 10 a.m. service but the 3,100 people who visited the church once but never returned over a period of five years. If only 20 percent of those visitors had become regular attenders, the church would be drawing more than a thousand people for worship on Sundays. Instead, the last time I checked, they were down to an average weekly attendance of 400.

Kicking the can down the road is a tactic that takes on countless forms. Churches become biblically illiterate when the Sunday school program evaporates after the really good Bible teacher leaves. Someone has to roll up his sleeves and invite people to Sunday school, but no one does it. The can gets kicked down the road. Church leadership has become so accustomed to kicking the can down the road that they insist on doing so, even in the face of becoming irrelevant, all because they prize the avoidance of upsetting anyone.

The problem comes down to leadership that claims a desire to draw people heavenward but isn't willing to listen to a few people complain because of the changes required to do so. It comes down to leaders who don't want to be bothered by a problem, so they sweep it under the carpet, to be dealt by somebody else some other day.

Perhaps you know of an organization that is paying the price for past leaders' decisions to kick the can down the road. Someone who kicks the can down the road is saying, "The moment of change is not now, no matter how much it may be needed." Churches have been putting off the moment of change for generations, and they wonder why they're shrinking.

Theodore Roosevelt said:

> Far better is it to dare mighty things, to win glorious triumphs even though checkered by failure, than to rank with those poor spirits who neither enjoy nor suffer much because they live in the gray twilight that knows neither victory nor defeat.

When you kick the can down the road and wait to make a decision, you've already made your decision. Doing nothing is a decision with dire consequences down the line. In the church, we routinely waive future success by settling for whatever spares us from any present pain. To change anything, there must come a moment when everyone takes a collective breath and says, "Okay, let's do it!"

⌒

Minding His Business Basic Principle:

*The absence of conflict in not a sign of good leadership;
it is a luxury that church leadership gives itself when it
refuses to ask people to step outside their comfort zone
and when it puts off the tough decisions for another day—
one that never dawns.*

CHAPTER 9

"SOMEONE WILL GET MAD"

Four words have stopped more ministry opportunities, diverted more meetings, and ended more great ideas than any other: "Someone will get mad." We are so accustomed to this statement, we even say it aloud in planning meetings, as if avoiding people's anger is a top goal for our organization.

Doubt is essential to the existence of faith. The opposite of faith is not doubt; it is surety. When things are certain, there is no room for doubt; faith is therefore rendered unnecessary. Church leaders need to be able to overcome their doubts and muster the courage to tell the aging singer screeching "O Holy Night" that it's time to sit down. To tell the counselor with halitosis to use breath mints. To fire the director of children's ministry who has proven ineffective.

How many people will get mad if we do what needs to be done? That's always the question. Whenever I hear somebody say, "Someone will get mad," I challenge him to make a list of the people he actually expects to offend. Often, only one or two people will voice their complaints.

Many leaders squander the promise of thousands of dollars in future revenue, miss out on dozens of opportunities to make disciples, and refuse to give free food to hungry people, all because they refuse to say to a few people, "I know this is going to make you uncomfortable, but this is what we're doing, anyway."

Whenever you hear somebody protest, "Someone will get mad," make it your responsibility to say, "Really? Make a list. Cite your data."

Those who conduct the business of church ministry have a God-given duty to be the voice of empirical reason at the table. Now, I want to be clear here: The foundation of the church is faith in Christ's redemptive work on the cross, and its primary goal is to see lives redeemed and transformed through salvation and through relationships in community. But someone has to be a standard-bearer for empirical reason, if for no other reason than to make sure it is not ignored. We cannot ignore the fruit, the evidence, of a shrinking church.

What is the evidence? Declining membership. The "salt" losing its savor. (See Matthew 5:13; Mark 9:50; Luke 14:34.) The bottom line is that, for fear of offending people, and in desperation to avoid conflict, we are allowing the church to fade into oblivion.

I was talking recently with the pastor of a 2,000-member congregation. The leadership had a big decision to make. A member of the team had played the "someone will get mad" card, and it had shaken up the pastor. When he called me for advice, I asked him, "Have you had ninety-nine percent of your people agree with every decision you've made?"

He said, "Oh, I wish!"

"So, even at a 99-percent parishioner satisfaction rate, no matter what you do, you get phone calls from at least 1 percent?"

"That's about right," he conceded.

"But getting twenty calls in a day feels like an avalanche."

"It seems like the sky has caved in on us," he said with a chuckle.

Of the 1 percent who complain, not all of them leave the church or take other action. Some people just need to get their frustration off their chest. Don't sacrifice the potential for future success just because the complaints of 1 percent of unhappy parishioners feels like a lot.

Again, too many church leaders try to avoid conflict at all costs, whether the church is large or small, the conflict major or miniscule. The fear that "someone might get mad" has caused the church in the western hemisphere to risk the loss of an entire generation.

Jesus assured His followers that they would suffer persecution for His sake. (See, for example, Mark 13:13.) As believers in Jesus, our very existence offends certain people. If we want to offend no one, we must say little and do even less. And with church attendance dwindling, often to the point where the church closes its doors, we're watching the body of Christ wither away to nothing, all because someone might get mad.

We can't afford to worry about offending our congregants, and we especially can't afford to fear angering our staff members. At a conference I attended with a bunch of pastors and church leaders, a young man who worked as a children's pastor advanced his belief that church staff should either be awarded comp time or be paid time-and-a-half or even double time for working during the Christmas season. A generation ago, everyone who chose church work knew he would be expected to work retail hours at low pay. Today, many church staffers expect to work banker's hours for high pay.

After his idea was shot down by several others, this young pastor regrouped and said that he didn't think the church staff should be expected to work between Christmas Eve and New Year's Day. When I attempted to explain the folly of his revised proposition, he cut me off and said, "We should not make staff work over Christmas. It's the church!"

I calmly replied, "Then I suggest you have your operations officer forward any calls from the people who are looking for their paychecks, and that you assume responsibility for paying the fees for the documents that don't get filed. Furthermore, the holidays can be a difficult time for many people. I suggest you record a voice mail greeting directing callers to phone the church down the street, instead. They will be open during the holidays, I'm sure, and will gladly take the calls."

Minding His Business **Basic Principle:**

The statement "Someone will get mad" is a subjective indication of a leader's desire to avoid dealing with a few unhappy people. In the light of our tendency to make decisions based on a desperation to avoid conflict, you should make a habit of reviewing the empirical evidence before deciding how to proceed.

CHAPTER 10

"FREE KITTENS" ARE NEVER FREE

A friend of mine has a T-shirt that says, "I was going to change the world, but then something shiny flew by." Shiny things fly past us every day, distracting even the wisest of us from time to time.

A national evangelistic organization was thrilled when a donor gave them a bus. It meant that the evangelist and the musicians would save tens of thousands of dollars they would have spent on airline tickets each month as they traveled the country, preaching the gospel.

The evangelist knew little about road tours, and he didn't think about the costs of having personnel endlessly on the road, the cost to their families, or the length of time he'd be out of the office. He didn't calculate the cost to administrate the thousands of people who partnered with the ministry while he was ministering to hundreds in a small town.

The staff spent an entire year working on a schedule that would allow the evangelistic team to drive seamlessly from one city to the next as they toured the country. On the day of the much-anticipated inaugural trip, everyone from the ministry gathered around the bus to watch it roll out of the parking lot. Before the bus even reached the freeway, someone knocked the curtain rod off the window. No one knew how to fix it, so the team just laughed as they waved at other travelers on the road. Their cheery mood was unfazed. "We've lost our privacy," they said, "but, hey, we still have a bus!"

At their first citywide meeting, one of the musicians received a call from home. His daughter had fallen and cracked her head open. He booked a ticket on the next flight out, and the other musicians made up for his absence. This was followed by three stops in other cities with effective ministry events, although the crowd sizes were not as large as they had anticipated. The budget shortfall would have to be made up in future cities. When they hit Florida, someone from the ministry office called the evangelist and asked if the team was going to be safe from the hurricane.

"What hurricane?" everybody wanted to know.

The hosts of their next several scheduled events ended up canceling in light of the forecasted storm. The team was far from home, and their next citywide meeting was over a week away. They were stuck. Then the hurricane changed its path, jeopardizing the entire Gulf region. The team steered the bus toward home, racing to outrun the storm. They opted to fly to the remaining cities on their tour, traveling home between each event. I was able to help them sell the bus, which is what they should have done immediately upon receiving it.

Church leaders must become experts at managing opportunity. It's critical to know what you know, as well as what you don't know. It's equally important to understand the costs incurred as a result of the things you don't know.

A friend of mine was eager to surprise his wife with the gift of a kitten he'd gotten for free from some neighborhood kids. This man knew nothing about cats and what the proper care of them entailed—vaccinations, deworming, neutering, and the like. A kitten from the local rescue shelter, which would have handled all those necessities, would have cost him $40. Yet he and his wife spent more than $400 on their "free" kitten.

Again, you must become an expert at managing opportunities. Someone on your staff may insist on the importance of recycling, for example. The question is, who is going to manage the church's recycling efforts? Sure, it may be important. But so are children. Are you going to divert resources that ought to be spent toward the children's ministry just so your church can maintain a recycling program? Opportunities need to be weighed and ranked in order of priority.

I did some consulting for an urban church of about 250 where the prominent members were all artsy people. They had proposed to the pastor the idea of converting the old house on the church property into a community center for the arts, as a method of outreach. They had been thrilled to receive a grant toward the project, and they'd quickly started refurbishing the building. They'd been giddy with excitement at the prospect of children learning the fine arts and church members having an opportunity to witness to local kids and their families.

Then, it finally dawned on them that someone would need to be on site to open the doors of the arts center at 8 a.m. every day and to staff the desk all day. It wasn't long before all the church volunteers were sucked into serving at the arts center. Other church programs suffered, and the staff was overburdened. By the time I came in to help, the arts center still looked great, but it was almost always closed due to a lack of adequate staff. The building created the illusion that they were serving the community, but they were digging a grave the whole time. They didn't manage their opportunities well.

Another mismanaged opportunity I witnessed was at a suburban church in the central valley of California. For thirty years, they had partnered with local schools in running a massive summer day camp—really a vacation Bible school in disguise. Each summer, about one thousand children attended, and scores of families joined the church every year as a direct result of the outreach.

One year, a prominent church member who believed in year-round education said, "Let's have a vocational VBS where we train youngsters with actual skills." Since most of the church members with the necessary expertise for teaching "actual skills" worked during the day, the staff scheduled the VBS sessions in the evenings. But they soon learned that most parents didn't want to be out and about at night, not to mention that kids preferred Bible stories to lessons on electrical circuits. And the regular pool of volunteers couldn't adjust to the time change or the switch in activities. The thirty-year streak of success came to an abrupt end.

It's crucial to keep the end goal in mind. I once had a friend ask my opinion on premillennialism versus postmillennialism. I responded that my opinion on the matter wasn't important. He wasn't pleased with my answer, so I asked him a question: "How does one's position on this matter help the church in fulfilling the Great Commission? Will settling a theological question between the two of us put more people in heaven?"

Remember, making disciples of all people is the reason the church exists. It's the "main thing." And for the church, keeping the main thing *as* the main thing *is* the main thing. Yet so much of what the church concerns itself with actually diverts time, talents, and resources away from the mission of proclaiming the gospel to a lost and hurting world.

Scripture says that we move from strength to strength. (See Psalm 84:7.) To do that, we have to recognize opportunities and manage them wisely. There are many good things a church can do; but, sometimes, the church spends time and effort on things that make its members feel good but have no heavenly value. And while these things may have a positive impact on people's earthly lives, if the church is not helping people prepare for the next life, it has failed to keep the main thing as the main thing.

〜

Minding His Business **Basic Principle:**

Remember that no gift is truly "free," and that not all good things are worth pursuing.

CHAPTER 11

STAY OUT OF HARM'S WAY, PART 1: RISK MANAGEMENT

Actuarial sciences is one of the hottest career choices right now. Why would anyone want to become an actuary? Because one can earn a lot of money doing the thankless job of measuring probability based on statistics and marrying it to the cost of failure in order to assess the value of risk. People hire actuaries because of the need to manage liability and calculate the cost of failure. For example, the odds of being struck by lightning are very low. Even so, I'm not going to play golf in Florida on a stormy afternoon in August, because, when I calculate the cost of failure, it's pretty high: my death.

Most people would consider an 83 percent chance of success to be pretty good. But if you look at the corresponding chance of failure, you have the same odds involved in playing Russian roulette—1 in 6, or about a 17 percent failure rate. However, in the game of Russian roulette, if you pull the trigger six times, the probability of failure is 100 percent; the cost is death. Given enough time, something bad will happen. In the case of church and nonprofit initiatives, at least the cost is "only" bankruptcy, albeit a slower, more painful kind of death.

When I'm hired to help an organization, one of the first things I do is check out their general liability insurance policy and seek out additional quotes. If you don't feel like reading an entire general liability insurance policy, competing insurance companies are happy to read the policy for you and tell you where you're exposed. Every church needs liability insurance because unexpected accidents are bound to happen.

Let's say that your church has a number of vehicles for which it decides to store gasoline in a shed, for the purpose of saving money by knocking out the middleman. But a storm can knock over a 200-gallon tank; and when the gas seeps into the groundwater, the church will be liable for millions of dollars of cleanup, not to mention environmental mitigation efforts. The additional cost of insurance to cover your church in the case of a fuel spill will probably eat up any savings you might have gained by storing the fuel yourself.

I received a call from a youth leader asking me to check out the contract with a rural park where he was hoping to take his students. The park offered horseback riding, rock climbing, a zip line, and waterfalls. And the contract absolved the park of all liability, even if the park was found to have been grossly negligent. The contract required the church to provide a certificate of insurance to protect the park and its staff from any lawsuits.

I told the youth leader to be sure to get that certificate of insurance before the outing. Simple, right?

When the youth leader found out that the certificate would cost $800—an amount that was high above his budget—he just told himself that nothing bad would happen, then grabbed the church credit card and took his students to the park. During their trip, one of the zip lines broke, and one of the teenage girls from the church fell and broke multiple bones. She had to undergo multiple surgeries and spend months recovering in the hospital. Fortunately, she recovered. Who was held liable? The church, of course. They had to pay for everything, on top of settling lawsuits with both the young girl's parents and the park. The entire ordeal cost the church an amount that totaled about a third of its annual budget.

When you review your insurance policy, make sure you really read it. Adding liability coverage for off-site events costs very little per year, and it is worth far more. Let's say that your church sponsors home-based Bible studies, and that, at one particular home meeting, a member has an allergic reaction to a peanut that was in a cookie he was served by the host and ultimately dies as a result. His family is legally entitled to go after the homeowner *and* your church. Your church may not be liable, but if the Bible study was announced during church services, and if members were encouraged to attend, your church could be found culpable; and culpability costs. And if your church does not have a rider specifically covering off-site events, it will end up paying a hefty price.

Get your policy from a reputable agent, and go over it thoroughly with him or her, making sure you understand every aspect.

A church on the East Coast established a thriving day care and implemented the "one or three" rule for the care and supervision of children, meaning that no person should ever be alone in a room with a child. There must be at least three people together; at no time should anyone be alone with a child, whether in the classroom or the restroom.

There were two volunteers teaching a class: a young woman from the community and a retired male schoolteacher from the congregation. One day, the young woman asked the male teacher to cover for her so that she could leave early to attend her child's school play. Even though her proposition was noncompliant with the "one or three" policy, the male teacher agreed. The woman told herself, *Nothing's going to happen.* That afternoon, he found himself left alone with one little girl whose parents were about fifteen minutes late in picking her up. After they came for their daughter, he locked up the classroom and headed home.

The next day, the church received a call from a mother in hysterics, insisting that her daughter had been sexually abused the previous evening when she'd stayed late at day care. Both the male and the female teacher were apologetic for having violated the "one or three" policy, but they said they were even sorrier for subjecting their church to a monumental crisis.

Scrambling, the church called its insurance company for help. The insurance company assured them that they would send out their own lawyer to walk them through the ordeal. What the church leadership hadn't noticed was the fine print in the insurance policy.

Most insurance policies are written in a way that favors the insurance company, and this church's policy was no exception. If you actually read your policy, you will usually find this to be true. But if you ask your insurance company, they will usually agree to change the policy for little additional cost, if any. The key is, you have to ask. And nobody at this church ever asked.

According to the policy, the church was protected against liability and theft; but under the section related to day care, the policy specified that in cases of alleged abuse, any felony conviction would render the coverage null and void.

The church, believing the insurance company to be working on their behalf, allowed the insurance attorney to settle the case. The attorney managed to get a settlement for the church, but he made sure there was a felony conviction against the male teacher, so that the insurance company didn't have to pay a dime.

Now, I would not be surprised if day care staffers at that church had violated the "one or three" policy many times over the years. The truth is, the head of the day care was such a pushover that she almost never addressed policy violations, let alone administered discipline for them. On the witness stand, when asked if she ever ignored violations by her staff of the "one or three" policy, the head of the day care responded, "We have cared for thousands of children over decades with not one incident or complaint of abuse. We are all like family. We love these children as our own. I never would have dreamed that this could ever happen."

That day care no longer exists. Neither does the church that sponsored it.

The head of the day care, and the church leadership overall, had let too many things slip through the cracks. For example, the church policy requiring all church staff—including day care supervisors—to submit to a background check was ignored in the case of the male day care worker, who, as it turns out, had been convicted of sexually abusing a child fifteen years prior in a different state. Had the church enforced its own policies, this entire debacle could have been avoided, and they might still be operating a successful day care and church today.

Most pastors are not schooled in contract law or liability management, and so the extent of liability management at most churches usually goes only as far as the pastor's anecdotal estimate of the probability that something bad will happen, with little or no consideration of the cost the church will incur if it does.

Furthermore, these risks are usually taken with an assumption that the pastor's anecdotal perception of the church's liability coverage is correct. In churches, this behavior is considered normal. In business, this behavior is considered reckless.

~

Minding His Business Basic Principle:

Given enough time, bad things are bound to happen. Enforce all your policies and read all your contracts.

PART II:

MONEY

CHAPTER 12

TREAT HIS MONEY LIKE YOUR MONEY

I once accepted a temporary assignment at a megachurch to help a pastor I'd known for years. He was a tremendous man behind the pulpit, astute in his dealings, and a natural people person. He was clearly committed to accomplishing the purpose for which God had put him on the planet. It was a pleasure just to know him.

The pastor called me because the staff of his well-run church had ballooned to well over 200, and something in the financial reports troubled him. He was having a hard time justifying how much of the budget was devoted toward the running of the church, and how little of it went toward missions and community outreaches. He wasn't concerned about overall expenditures; he just wanted me to find a way to transition some of the church's operating budget, and its personnel, in a direction that was more outreach-oriented.

When I reviewed the church's finances, I understood what he was talking about. They had significant land holdings, the congregation was filled with faithful tithers, and the balance sheet was robust. The financials were in so good a shape that a business-person in any sector would have been proud to present them to a bank. But it was also apparent that the majority of expenditures went toward maintaining what the congregation had built, and not nearly as much spent on building more—say, planting additional churches or helping the local or global community.

My team and I started to drill down into each financial avenue to see what we could change while creating minimal disruptions in operations. Almost immediately, we started freeing up cash and personnel to be devoted to outreach efforts. One thing I noticed was that every ministry leader carried a church credit card; so, while I was looking at the big numbers, I also paid attention to the "little numbers." I have found, over the years, that the little numbers often add up to be big numbers.

The youth ministry had an enormous budget at its disposal. A young, vibrant pastor led an enormous group of young people that was larger than many church congregations. I identified plenty of ways to reduce the budget, such as by eliminating free T-shirts and other giveaways and instead having the kids pay for them (at cost, not to make a profit). I also suggested hiring someone to repair the outdated equipment in the recreation area rather than replacing it with new equipment, as the church had been prepared to do. I even researched and selected a trusted company of competent people to handle the repairs.

The youth pastor started avoiding me.

Although I approach every new relationship by giving the other person the benefit of the doubt, I soon noticed a charge on the youth pastor's credit card statement for which, try as I might, I couldn't find a good explanation. I called him in for a brief meeting.

"I took the youth ministry staff and their spouses or signifi-cant others out for a nice dinner as a way of saying thank you," he explained.

I raised my eyebrows. "To one of the finest restaurants in town?"

He shrugged. "Just my way of letting them know how valuable they are to the program."

"Yet, they are on staff," I reminded him. "Every paycheck assures them of their value."

"I felt they deserved something more."

He was a nice guy. A soulwinner. Completely genuine. But I couldn't imagine him spending his own money at that establishment. The only reason he'd selected it as a way of saying "thank you" to those staff members was because he wanted to dine there.

I let him go with a smile, and then gave it some thought. When the next payday rolled around, I asked the accounting department for the youth pastor's check. I put it in the desk of the temporary office they'd given me. When he approached the accounting department and asked for his check, they told him I had it.

"Don," he said as he entered my office. "I didn't get my check."

"I know," I said, without looking up.

"Well, I need it. It's payday, and I have bills."

"I know," I said, still not looking up.

He started getting agitated. "Don, when can I get my check? It's my money!"

I finally met his gaze. "You're upset, right? Your face is red, and your hands are shaking. All I want to say is that I'd like to see that same focus, drive, and passion when you're dealing with the church's money."

He hung his head.

"You're a great guy," I told him as I handed him his paycheck. "You're doing a great work. And so am I. Please don't get mad at me for asking you to treat the church's money the way you treat your own money."

In the end, the church did expand its evangelism efforts, and the youth pastor remained a vibrant part of its missional outreach to young people.

⌒

Minding His Business Basic Principle:

Be as passionate about minding God's money as you are your own money.

CHAPTER 13

HONOR THE "WIDOW'S MITE"

Ministry leaders are responsible to do what Jesus did—to watch over ministry finances. Jesus watched people giving in the temple and commended a widow for the great sacrifice she had made. Though she gave only two coins (known as a "mite"), she gave all that she had. (See Mark 12:41–44; Luke 21:1–4.) In the same way, we have to honor the level of sacrifice that people make to support the spread of the gospel and the life of the church.

I was once working in a part of the country where there were probably more millionaires per square mile than perhaps any-where else in the world, outside of Dubai. That meant that there were also dozens of incredible restaurants that catered to the elite. My wedding anniversary was coming up, so I asked my wife to fly in and join me on my business trip, and told her we'd splurge on dinner at one of these fine establishments. Our annual family budget allows for occasional indulgences, and it felt great to be able to treat my bride to a special meal.

We dressed in our finest clothes and made our way to the res-taurant, excited to be doing something so extravagant to celebrate our wonderful years together. When we walked in, I was more than a little surprised to see two staff members from the ministry I had been helping, seated at a table having dinner together. I knew their salaries—believe me, they couldn't have afforded to dine there, especially if it wasn't to celebrate some momentous occasion.

They didn't see me, so I just waited while I tried to determine what to do about it. Sure enough, when that month's expense reports came rolling in, one of the two staff members had included a receipt for the $300 "business dinner" he'd shared with the other staffer. According to IRS regulations, the amount was taxable to the employee, and I couldn't believe their disregard for the sacrificial donations people had made to the ministry.

The ministry where they served was located in a working-class neighborhood. What if the grocers or plumbers in the congregation heard that these staffers had used ministry money to cover their dinner at an expensive restaurant?

I pulled aside the staffer who had included the dinner on his expense report and asked that he tell the rest of the staff about the expense at the next meeting.

"I don't need to do that," he insisted. "It's not a big deal."

"If it's not a big deal, then why don't you want to do it?"

"C'mon, man," he pleaded.

Then I tried a different approach. "You know, the ladies' group that meets on Thursday mornings to pray for the staff is made up predominantly of widows and singles, most of whom live on a fixed income. Why don't you just go and tell them how great the dinner was and thank them for paying for the extravagant meal?"

"Stop." His face turned red. "What are you doing?"

"Can you just be honest?" I asked. "If I said that I'd pay you five hundred dollars to go tell those ladies a joke, you'd do it in a heartbeat. The truth is, you're ashamed of what you did, because you know it was wrong."

He ate the expense and learned the lesson.

A litmus test I use to determine the righteousness of a choice I am considering is to ask myself, *Would I be willing to do or say whatever I am contemplating in front of my entire church congregation?* If I would not want my thoughts or my decision put up on the big screen for all to see, it is probably not righteous.

I knew a ministry leader who loved to play golf and kept a country club membership. The problem was, he ministered to a low-income, urban constituency. One day, he invited me to play a round of golf with him and his cronies.

I thought about my sons. I hadn't grown up with any exceptional role models, but I desperately wanted to be an exceptional role model for them. And I wondered if I could, in good conscience, tell the people who made sacrificial contributions to the church that I'd taken $195 of their money to play a round of golf. I ended up declining the pastor's invitation.

If you're weighing a decision that relates to money, just imagine telling your entire congregation how you spent it. If you would be comfortable doing so, then it's probably a right and a righteous thing. We have to trust the Holy Spirit to give us discernment in this area.

⌒

Minding His Business Basic Principle:

The sacrifice of the widow shows us the importance of spending money wisely.

CHAPTER 14

WHEN IN DOUBT, BID IT OUT

Palm trees swayed outside the window of the temporary office I'd been assigned in a growing church. The scent of flowers came in on a breeze, making my mug of burnt coffee smell even worse by comparison. I sat there, pondering how it was that some church offices brewed some of the worst coffee, when the beverage was first popularized by monks and had been making an appearance at church socials for centuries. After about half a minute of such musings, I returned my attention to the document on the desk in front of me. I felt like I was sitting in old, worn-out territory that felt worse than the coffee tasted. Different church, same problem.

I had been brought in by the church board to ensure that there was forward movement in this growing congregation of young families. They wanted to construct a playground as a solution, albeit a temporary one, to the problem of overcrowding in the children's ministry classrooms. Sandy, the children's minister, named one of the children's fathers as the "perfect choice" to build it.

It might have been the coffee, but I suspect it was really the bid submitted by the "perfect choice" that made my stomach turn that morning. I had built a backyard play gym for my sons when they were small. It wasn't industrial-grade construction, mind you; yet the bid on the paper in front of me made it seem as if we wanted to rebuild the Pentagon.

In the staff meeting, I had to go toe-to-toe with the already beleaguered children's minister, who was dealing with too many children for the space she'd been provided. Sandy insisted that the man she had in mind for the job could have a wonderful playground built in three weeks' time. It was clear that she had all but told him the job was his. Her heart was in the right place, wanting immediate relief for the kids; but she hadn't done her homework.

I asked the pastor to give me a week to do further research before he gave Sandy's recommendation the go-ahead to do the job. The pastor agreed, and Sandy sulked.

Over the next week, I approached three different local construction companies, none of which was familiar with the church. The bids they provided were all over the place, but the lowest dollar amount was what I'd originally hoped the cost would be—more than a backyard set, but a fraction of the first bid.

Before I brought my findings to the pastor, I needed to do a little more digging. If the man Sandy had recommended had been giving the church $100,000 per year, let's say, then overpaying him by a few thousand dollars for a construction project wasn't going to hurt the church finances as much as offending him by declining his services would. Yet, if he'd been investing that much on an annual basis, he might be the first to want to save money.

The question was, would the money we would pay him cycle back into the church? If so, it could mean a lot of people getting to heaven because of his ongoing support. If not, then how could we claim to be good stewards while spending close to three times as much as another available bid? That could mean a lot of people being kept *out* of heaven because of the outreach programs we would not be able to afford to do because we'd spent three times too much on a playground. Remember, price is not the same as cost.

It wasn't that I was accusing Sandy's recommendation of being a crook. Maybe he didn't have the same equipment or resources as the company that had put forth the lower bid. Maybe he was in between jobs and just wanted to be able to retain his employees, lest they start looking for other jobs. Or maybe his employees were more highly skilled and, therefore, more highly paid. There could have been dozens of reasons for the price difference.

I asked the church bookkeeper to show me this man's record of giving, which I then took to the pastor's office. We compared all the bids and assessed how the pastor thought the young father would react if turned down for the job. Then we called Sandy into the office.

"We don't believe we can go with his bid," the pastor told her. "But if we go with this other bid, we could potentially hire some paid nursery workers instead of depending on volunteers. Wouldn't that be a bigger help in the long run?"

"When can the playground be installed?" Sandy asked.

"Within the month," I told her.

Sandy beamed. She took it up on herself to contact the man she'd recommended and explain to him that his nursery-aged child would soon receive even better care because of the way we were deciding to appropriate the funds.

In the end, the church never did improve the coffee they served, but the playground went up quickly and professionally. No programs had to be cut, and they even added a nursery employee. Sandy was thrilled. And the young father, to my knowledge, has raised his children in that church.

Getting competitive bids takes time and planning. Unfortunately, in most churches, decisions tend to be made at the last minute, meaning there isn't time to get multiple bids. But forgoing the bid process is not good stewardship. I wonder how many ministry and church staffers who don't ask for competitive bids with ministry money would walk onto a car lot and purchase a vehicle for themselves without getting any price comparisons, either online or at another dealership. We are careful with our own money; let's give God's money the same consideration, if not better.

◡〜

Minding His Business **Basic Principle:**

When considering any purchase, here is the recommended rule of thumb:

Small churches: Get at least two bids to spend $1,000 or more. Get at least three bids to spend $2,500 or more.

Large churches: Get at least two bids to spend $2,500 or more. Get at least three bids to spend $5,000 or more.

CHAPTER 15

YOU GET WHAT YOU INSPECT, NOT WHAT YOU EXPECT

I landed in a large southern city and rented a car at the airport. Flying, driving, working—it was routine. I had been called by a pastor friend to look over his church's financials after the board had asked for a second opinion on some budgetary items.

When I returned from my last trip, to Indianapolis, my wife had asked me what the city was like now, since she hadn't been there in years. I told her, "It looks the same as Philly, which looks like Boston, which looks like Seattle—all I saw was a hotel, a rental car, and the inside of a church office."

The pastor I was visiting had the receptionist usher me straight into his office. He wanted to show me around the facilities, and no wonder. They were magnificent. The large congregation had built a real hub for the community it served.

We toured the church school classrooms and the cavernous sanctuary, and then he drove me by golf cart out to the athletic complex. It was a dream facility, with courts for basketball, volley-ball, and tennis, and fields for soccer, football, and baseball.

"All you need is a pool!" I said, half joking.

He pointed to the vacant plot of land beyond the fields. "We own all that, too," he said. "That's where we'll build the aquatic center. Just be sure to come here on Saturday, because this place is packed!"

For the next couple of days, I drove back and forth from the hotel to the church office, where I pored over the financial reports and membership records. On Saturday, I decided to split my time, starting on records in the morning and then heading to the office mid-morning so I could see exactly what that pastor head meant by "packed."

I had to pay a fee to enter the athletic facility, but it was very reasonable. I noticed that the children paid to play, and the parents paid to watch, but the prices were so low that anyone living in that particular community could afford it. Memberships were also available, with the perk of a complimentary T-shirt.

The best part was, the place was packed, by anyone's defini-tion, just as the pastor said it would be. Children of all ages and their parents were climbing over every inch of that property. There were concession booths selling beverages at reasonable prices that would turn a profit for the church.

Now here is a congregation that has found a relevant way to serve the community, I thought. My next thought was, *I wonder how much profit they're turning in this one department alone.*

In the church office that afternoon, I finished scrutinizing the department I'd been exploring, then moved on to the records related to the athletic center. The pastor was so proud of what they'd accomplished, and for good reason. Now it was time to see how it fared financially.

The numbers were staggering. That one ministry alone was responsible for a $400,000 deficit since it opened. Their budget had been in the red ever since. I opened a new Excel spreadsheet and started my own calculations, based on the number of people I estimated having seen at the complex that afternoon, how many memberships (and free T-shirts) they had sold, and how much the concession booth should have been bringing in.

On Monday, I was all smiles as I asked to see the receipts from the previous Saturday. The athletic director had been a big star in Division I college basketball. The community loved her, and the church felt fortunate to have her on staff. But she didn't submit any report.

I called my wife and told her I'd be staring at hotel and office walls for another week, and that she shouldn't expect me home anytime soon.

For the next three days, I kept asking to see the receipts. Finally, the athletic director came to the office where they'd set me up, defiant and angry. "What's your problem?" she demanded. "I've been doing this job just fine without you. We don't need help collecting the money!"

Right then, I knew that a situation that had been mildly unpleasant thus far was about to get a lot worse. There was no way to get to the bottom of the issue without upsetting the athletic director. I approached the pastor and the CFO and proposed that the accounting staff show up unannounced at the athletic complex the following Saturday to collect all the money earned that day.

They approved my plan. When we arrived the following weekend, the athletic director was livid. The fields and courts were just about as busy as they'd been the previous Saturday. Normally, the weekend receipts totaled close to $2,000. That Saturday, the accounting staff collected over $4,000. Why had the profits suddenly doubled?

I went back to the office and started looking at the record of T-shirt purchases alone. The church had paid for about two thousand T-shirts per year, but there were sales receipts for only about 600 of them. I figured there had to be either a big pile of money or a big pile of T-shirts somewhere, and I wanted to see it.

When we finished the investigation, we discovered that the athletic director had skimmed a total of $150,000 off the church's profits. I don't know at what point she started pocketing money on a weekly basis, but at some point, she realized that no one ever checked on her. No one ever followed up. No one inspected her work. And that small realization is where big problems begin.

I once ran a printing company, and one of our customers was a local distributor of Pepsi products. One day, I received a complaint from the distributor that the blue in our Pepsi ads was not the right shade. It turns out that "Pepsi blue" is a very specific hue, and "close" does not cut it with Pepsi. It was too light.

Now, we had run these ads for years without any problems. After some investigation, we isolated the problem to a printing press on the third shift. I decided to drop in unannounced at 3 a.m. What I found was a printing press running with no pressman to be found. About an hour later, the pressman came walking in, stinking of liquor. I fired him on the spot. What I later found out was that everyone but me knew that this pressman drank on the job and often left his press running to go to the bar down the street. When the word got out to the rest of the plant that the boss was pulling "surprise inspections," quality went up, and waste went down, almost overnight.

The question is not "Why did quality improve so fast?" The correct question is, "Why did the quality lapse in the first place?" As leaders, we set the standard. If we accept mistakes without correction, people will make more mistakes. If we tolerate poor behavior, people will behave badly. By inspecting the work of those we lead, we communicate to them that we care about results and quality, and so should they.

Ever since my "surprise inspection" during the third shift, I no longer needed to show up at that time every night to ensure that quality work was done. Just the fact that the pressmen knew I might show up at any time was enough to get Pepsi blue back to looking like Pepsi blue.

~

Minding His Business Basic Principle:

You get what you inspect, not what you expect. If you don't inspect, you should expect to be disappointed.

CHAPTER 16

HONEST PEOPLE DEMAND AUDITS

Counting church money is important. Sometimes, it is the most important thing you can do—especially in the case of suspected embezzlement or an audit. The rest of the time, it's just a mundane matter of good stewardship. The leader's responsibility is to ensure that incoming money is accounted for and that expenditures are monitored. Someone has to pay attention to those details.

I was called in to help a church of about 1,500 members. The annual budgeted amount for accounting expenditures exceeded $100,000. This seemed exorbitant to me, but I soon learned that the accountant, Susan, was loved and trusted by everyone. No matter what we asked, if it involved money, the staff would say, "Let's call Susan."

So, I started calling Susan—first for one thing, and then for another. At first, she was very friendly and quick to respond. But when I asked her to send me the church's financials to review, I immediately noticed the absence of any balance sheet—pretty much the most important document when it comes to reviewing an organization's finances. It is on the balance sheet that the income statements and the bank statements must reconcile (balance). Without a balance sheet, an accountant can make the numbers be anything he or she wants them to be, and no one will know.

So, I called Susan again. This time, I couldn't get her to return my calls. That's almost always a sign that something's amiss. I wondered what it might be. I looked at the records I'd been given to see about Susan's attendance and giving.

"Pastor," I said in a private meeting, "I know we all know and love Susan, but look at her attendance record. She hasn't been to church in a year!"

"Oh?" the pastor said. "I knew she had been really busy, but I didn't realize it had been that long."

"She also hasn't given a penny in a year."

"Oh!" the pastor said. "I'll invite her out for a cup of coffee."

After her meeting with the pastor, Susan finally called me back.

I asked her once more for the balance sheet.

She wanted to know if I was questioning her integrity.

I hadn't been, until she asked.

As I explained, I approach every situation ready to give the other person the benefit of the doubt. I generally presume that people in ministry are intending to do good. But whenever a simple question about a process or a procedure prompts someone to become defensive about his or her integrity, competency, and the like, I can't help but become a bit suspicious.

This is an important lesson for every ministry professional to learn. If you call for an audit of a dishonest person, he will almost invariably change the subject to make it a question of character.

And if you question the character of an honest person, he will demand an audit to prove the absence of any wrongdoing.

When we conducted an informal internal audit at the church, Susan and her assistant were very upset. What we found was that, while they were absolutely honest, they were also absolutely inefficient and, in some areas, incompetent.

Never having transitioned to the digital record-keeping methods available, Susan's assistant was constantly bogged down in paperwork. They were still using green ledger paper, if you can believe it. There was no way to keep up with the many transactions involved in a church of that size, so Susan had hired an assistant to work solely for the church, performing tasks manually that should have been done electronically. As a result, the accounting bills being charged to the church had risen over the years to the huge fees being paid.

Since I'd uncovered the issue, I felt an obligation to find a solution. We soon hired a competent firm that used every digital method available to expedite transactions, reporting methods, and communications. They charged the church about $55,000 per year—a savings of 45 percent.

We quickly absorbed that savings and funneled it into outreach activities. For $10,000, we hosted a youth event that resulted in hundreds of young people committing their lives to Christ. We gave $5,000 to the local food bank. We invested $10,000 in the development of a new Web site designed to convert visitors into members. And by the end of a year, there was still a surplus of $20,000 because of the dollars saved and earned.

Susan and her assistant were not bad people, but they had been napping in the hammock of everyone's trust. They knew that the church leadership wasn't going to ask hard questions. No one doubted the hours they reported working, so they kept working the same number of hours without making any efforts to improve efficiency and reduce costs. I compared their behavior to someone swimming with a pocketful of rocks. It can be done, but why would anyone want to try it?

I have worked with hundreds of nonprofit organizations, and most of the accounting problems I've encountered have been the result of employees who know that the leadership won't ask hard questions. And why is this? Because the leadership doesn't know what questions to ask. When those giving oversight to an organization don't know much about business, it requires a lot of trust, and there's a price to pay for that. An audit is the fastest way to ascertain if finances are being handled properly by the responsible parties. Just remember, honest people never fear an audit.

∽

Minding His Business Basic Principle:

An audit can uncover dishonest employees, archaic systems, and wasteful methods. Call for an audit anytime you suspect any of these three issues might be occurring in your organization. Call for one even if you don't!

CHAPTER 17

NOT A HINT OF IMPROPRIETY

Churches, charities, and similar nonprofit organizations are public trusts that exist for the public good. In order for them to fulfill their purpose, there must be accountability and transparency. To put off or avoid inspections due to anxiety over uncovering something or offending someone will only make matters worse. The absence of accountability is a breeding ground for temptation.

I have a few ironclad rules that I live by, one of which is that I refuse to allow even a hint of impropriety from myself, from my staff, and from any situation in which I'm involved. Imagine if someone were to say to you today, "Prove that you've never cheated on your spouse." What would you offer as proof? How do you prove something didn't happen? It's impossible. When faced with certain accusations, a spotless reputation may be your only proof.

At a church where I was called in to help with some membership marketing, there was a young pastor who was the quintessential "people person." Young, fit, and funny, he flashed a five-hundred-watt smile about a hundred times a day. And, he was a hugger. Young or old, male or female, single or married—it didn't matter; he was always hanging on or hugging someone.

When I'd been working with the church long enough that I felt comfortable asking a favor from the accountant, I requested a couple hundred bucks from the building maintenance budget for a special project.

Next, I went to the pastor and said, "I'm about to save you a lawsuit, a lot of bad press, and a big headache. I have the money appropriated and a builder ready to come tomorrow to cut a hole and install a window in the office door of the 'hugging machine' pastor. All I need is your okay." Then I went back to worked on the marketing campaign.

Prudence demands that you not let yourself or any member of the staff sit in an enclosed office one-on-one with any person for any reason. You cannot inspect what you cannot see. Even if you never give in to temptation, you cannot hope to prove your innocence when a crazy person accuses you of impropriety "behind closed doors" and you have no eyewitnesses to speak in your defense.

Another one of my ironclad rules is that I refuse to either live in fear or engender fear in others. In the organizations where I serve, the only people who fear me are those who are lazy or are doing something wrong.

I also refuse to work with people I don't trust—I must be able to trust the leaders I serve—and I refuse to give anyone a reason not to trust me.

For about a year, I flew routinely in and out of a southern city where I was helping to reorganize the operations at a large church. We trimmed millions of dollars from the budget and eventually improved their credit enough that they secured a credit line as high as they needed it to be at the new bank I connected them to. We also requested competitive bids for contracts from various vendors and hired new ones in lieu of many of those the church had been working with for years.

The savings were substantial. The board was thrilled. But some of the former vendors who had been replaced started bad-mouthing me to the church staff members, and their comments filtered upward.

In a meeting with the pastor, the CEO, and the CFO, a leader called me out.

"I understand you're taking kickbacks from the new vendors we're doing business with," he said point-blank.

I pulled out my checkbook and started writing. (Now, none of my three sons could tell you the location of his checkbook; but, because I'm from a different generation, I happen to carry mine in my briefcase.) I then slid a check across the table to the pastor.

"Here you go," I said. "Here is the total amount of money you have paid me to bring the church to the state of robust financial health it enjoys today. I demand an audit of every vendor. If you find any impropriety at all, I won't rest until you cash that check. But if you find none, then you can give me back the check and thank the Lord for bringing you such an honest guy to help with the church's finances."

I'm not offended when someone wants to inspect my work. No one who prizes transparency should be offended by inspections. When my children were young, I made it clear that I expected them to be able to sit on the edge of my bed every evening and tell me everything they had done that day. And I hold myself to the same standard. I am committed to making my conduct such that I would be completely comfortable sitting on the edge of any of my sons' beds and telling him about it without experiencing even a hint of shame.

Audits are a lot like locks. Locks are put in place to keep honest people honest. The front door of your house can be kicked in without much effort. You lock it only to keep honest people honest. But a real criminal, if he's intent on getting in, is going to get in, no matter what.

The purpose of an audit is to protect your organization by making sure it isn't easy for anyone on your staff to become a criminal. Even an honest person can become dishonest for a while. A person who struggles with an addiction to alcohol can spend forty years sober, then fall off the wagon for six months. A good person can fall on hard financial times and give in to the pressure and temptation to embezzle. Before you know it, you're out $100,000, and the reputation of your staff's family is forever ruined.

As sinful mortals, we are liable to fail and to fall victim to temptation. Part of doing kingdom work is to guard against temptation and give *"not even a hint of* [impropriety]*"* (Ephesians 5:3). We owe it to the people we lead to create a system and culture where impropriety is not permitted to exist.

◠

Minding His Business **Basic Principle:**

Create a culture of transparency where impropriety cannot exist.

CHAPTER 18

THE CHURCH IS NOT A BUSINESS

The church is not a business. The church just conducts business. And for a church to conduct business effectively, there needs to be at least one person on staff there who knows what he's doing.

An urban church in the old downtown section of a West Coast city was nearing its hundredth birthday. Elders from a previous generation had had the foresight to establish an endowment for the beautiful building they had constructed, now covered in ivy. The endowment was intended to preserve and maintain the church building so that it could be used to spread the gospel for generations to come.

The houses in the surrounding area fell into disrepair over the years. Aging residents passed away, and their children either sold the houses or turned them into inexpensive rental properties. After several decades of this declining trend, a swell of urbanization hit the decrepit neighborhood, and a new generation of young people started buying the old houses and fixing them up.

It wasn't long before the church congregation began to expand, and the board called me in to help them navigate this new, exciting growth spurt. It was obvious to everyone that the first step was to do some renovations to the building. It was equally obvious that they needed to begin in the children's area, located in the church basement—a dark, wet, moldy mess of a place. No parent in his right mind would have permitted his child to go down there, unless he or she was dressed in a child-sized hazmat suit.

The church was just starting its uptick in membership, but a corresponding uptick in income had yet to happen. There was no cash available to renovate the children's area, but I was certain that the income would grow once the project was complete.

It didn't take me long to realize that there was no donor base from which an adequate amount of money could be raised. The older members either were living on fixed incomes or had exhausted their reserves during the years of economic decline; the new members were not yet invested enough to entertain a request of significant financial giving. So, we turned to the endowment to see how it might be put to use.

We soon learned that the endowment intended to preserve the church's brick walls had virtually *become* a brick wall itself. One generation had created the endowment, leaving the next generation to figure out how to manage it. A well-meaning member of the church board had decided to put the endowment funds into long-term bonds during an era when people believed that their principal was protected and that they'd receive it back later after earning interest. Unfortunately, that board member did not understand the ins and outs of bond ratings and bond discounts. He didn't know that bonds with high rates of return have lower bond ratings and are therefore riskier, often incurring penalties for early withdrawals. Furthermore, in an environment of rising interest rates, the surrender value on the bonds went down. Plainly put, this board member was asked to perform a business function (investment) for the church that he was not qualified to perform.

It is crucial that the people making financial decisions on behalf of the church be experts in the field. I would not expect a church pastor to be familiar with bond discount rates, but if someone suggests investing the church's money in bonds, he had better know what he is doing. In the case of this particular church, if they were to cash out the bonds in a market of rising interest rates, they wouldn't get all their money back. Only if they allowed the long-term bonds to mature, or if interest rates fell, would they get their principal back. They needed the money immediately, but the bonds would not mature for another ten to twenty years. If they cashed out their corporate bonds, due to the stipulations of early withdrawal, they would forfeit portions of their principal.

Someone had probably assured the early church board members that bonds were the safest route to take, and so those members made a long-term financial decision based on their personal comfort level with the apparent risk involved. Yet they lacked the knowledge and experience necessary to qualify them to make such a decision. And the misinformed decision they made ended up preventing the church from being able to fulfill the very purpose of the endowment. The early church congregation had raised all that money for nothing, as it were.

The money was sitting there, but it couldn't be accessed without the church's having to forfeit a sizable chunk of the principal. The congregation could not raise the money for renovations, nor could they cash in the bonds; thus, the musty basement remained the only place to put the children. The congregation had once been a large, thriving church, and it could have experienced a resurgence, if only they hadn't been prevented from seizing an opportunity to improve their facilities. The pastor hung in there and tried everything he could think of to overcome the circumstances, but the young families just didn't want to raise their children in that dank, decrepit basement. Soon, the pastor resigned, and the church became an empty shell of what it once was.

From a business perspective, hundreds of thousands of dollars of potential revenues were lost because the church couldn't get the liquidity. Worse, from a spiritual perspective, generations of families were lost because the church could not function.

The root cause was that someone had invested money without knowing what he was doing.

Another church I worked with was located in a poor urban neighborhood where nobody in the congregation could get approved for a credit card. Someone came along selling prepaid debit cards. This individual was backed by several big banks and boasted endorsements from a number of notable Christian leaders. For every transaction, he promised that the church would make money. The company's records showed a very good track record.

No one on the church board thought to ask, "What if he's wrong? Whom will the parishioners blame if it doesn't work? What if the program goes bankrupt? Is it protected by the FDIC?"

The prepaid debit cards took off faster than the issuing company anticipated, and it couldn't manage the growth. Sure enough, the company went bankrupt. Many of the congregants of that church had been putting money on those credit cards every week and had also been saving money in the corresponding accounts. Everyone who had his money invested in the cards lost money.

Doing "due diligence" may feel like the opposite of "walking by faith." But business is business. Call the minister when you need ministry; call a businessperson you trust when you need to transact business.

Minding His Business **Basic Principle:**

People making business decisions that impact the church or congregation need to know what they're doing. Hire people with proven track records and solid reputations to conduct the business of the church.

CHAPTER 19

BUSINESS IS A TESTIMONY

One of the easiest and simplest ways to convey your Christian testimony to your community is by conducting business well. And the easiest, simplest principle of conducting a business well is to pay your bills on time.

A giant church in a small town called me to help them develop a five-year budget. On my first couple of days in town, I made a morning stop at one of several coffee shops to gauge the spiritual temperature of the community and its impression of the church I had gone there to help. It didn't take me long to discover that most of the people didn't care for the church or its pastor.

When I dug into the church's financials, the first thing I noticed was that they were overpaying for even the most basic services.

One of my contacts was a businessman who knew people in the town, so I started calling the people from a list he gave me. After introducing myself and briefly summarizing the situation, I would say, "Can you help me out with this?"

"I'm not going to do business with that church!" was the universal response.

"Why?" I would press.

The common refrain was, in a nutshell, "They don't pay their bills."

Finally, I asked one of them, "Do they owe you money?"

"No."

"Have they ever owed you money?"

"No."

I went back through the church records. The strange thing was, the church had always paid its bills. It had always had the necessary cash on hand to cover its bills. The accounting department had a system in place that should have ensured every bill was paid. I couldn't figure it out.

Finally, I discovered that the church leaders themselves didn't understand the system. To them, purchase orders seemed like unimportant paperwork that was secondary to all their other duties. As a result, a bill would come to accounting, accounting would send it to the minister involved to write a purchase order (after the expenditure had been made), and the minister would leave it alone until he or she made an effort to catch up on "unimportant" paperwork, at which point it would be sent back to accounting—sometimes after several months had passed.

In the meantime, the church's reputation kept getting worse, and the accounting staff kept getting harried with collection calls.

"I'm going to take every collection call from here on out," I told the bookkeepers. "Don't try to talk to the people when I'm not here. Just forward me their contact information, and I'll call them back."

At the next staff meeting, I laid out what was happening. "Your order might be the only order that a vendor gets," I said. "If we don't pay the vendor, they can't make payroll. Your failure to honor the system affects more people than you probably realize."

To me, it was a kingdom principle, and the staff all came to see it that way. The pastor backed me up, using Scripture to explain how difficult it is to recover one's reputation once it has been soiled.

Then he asked me to make some closing remarks to the discussion.

"From now on, I'm personally taking all the collection calls that come to this church," I told everyone. Then, sweeping my gaze across the room to catch the eye of as many staffers as possible, I said, "God help the person who doesn't fill out the paperwork and makes us pay our bills late."

Within six months, there were no more collection calls coming in.

Yet, there was still more to do. Once I knew the system was working, I had the church administrator send a letter to all the vendors to tell them, in essence, "Here are our payment discount policies. If you want to be paid within ten days, give us a 5 percent discount. If you want to be paid within thirty days, give us a 2 percent discount. If you want to be paid within sixty days, you can expect payment in full."

Most vendors chose to get the money right away, but several bigger companies agreed to the 60-day term. Over time, as the church administrator got to know the representatives from all the companies, he followed my recommendation to call them up, give them his personal cell phone number, and tell them to feel free to call with any concerns—proof that they were committed to being the best customer that vendor had ever worked with.

Over time, the local businesspeople started asking vendors that worked with the church, "Are you really doing business with them?"

The vendors would say, "Yes, that church is one of the best customers we've ever worked with."

When I followed up with the church a year later, I found that many local companies were vying with one another for the church's business. The administrator had worked to build relationships with the business owners and introduced them to the pastor, who, as a result, was getting to know most of the leading businesspeople in town.

But there was even more to do. I encouraged the church to continue developing relationships and to turn some of them into partnerships. Soon, the church was writing grants and proposals and receiving funds and sponsorships from area businesses for community outreach projects. Within a couple of years, that church looked like the spiritual beacon it had always wanted to be.

If you're a pastor or church leader of any kind, you would do well to build relationships with as many local businesses as possible. It's simpler than you think.

❧

Minding His Business **Basic Principle:**

The easiest and simplest testimony of a church is the way it conducts business. Be the best customer your vendors have ever had, and pay your bills on time.

CHAPTER 20

GOD'S WILL PROVIDES

Wh_hen the pastor or other church leader is in the center of
God's will, God will provide. It's a strange thing for a business
leader to watch, especially when you feel like sticking your foot in
the middle of a situation where God intends to work a miracle. It's
only by the grace of God that I've kept my mouth shut on those
occasions and allowed the miracle to unfold.

It happened once when a dear friend who ran a large ministry came upon hard times. I loved this man like a brother and
would have followed him to the ends of the earth. He called me
one morning in complete distress, and before we hung up, I had
purchased an airline ticket to his city for the following day.

When I arrived at his office, I found him with his wife and his
executive staff, all huddled around a table discussing what to do.
Everyone looked worried. The atmosphere was so brittle, it felt as
if I might break something just by walking in.

My friend introduced me to some of the staff members I hadn't
met, since it had been years since I'd last been to his headquarters.
He told them that we had known each other for a long time and

that he valued my judgment in matters of business, and then he rehashed for me the scenarios they had discussed and the possible solutions they'd explored. He also gave me a financial statement to look over. Judging from what I saw, I was not optimistic about our chances of finding a way to turn the ministry around. *They've waited too long*, I thought. *It's going to take a miracle to get this boat upright again.*

As our meeting progressed, various staff members offered their own points of view. All of the ideas were valid, it's just that none of them would solve the problem. Fresh off a last-minute flight, I was cold to the situation and feeling helpless. I had nothing to add. The leader finally said, "Let's just pray awhile."

He lifted his voice, and it was one of those prayer times that was nothing short of heavenly. When he spoke to his Father, it was as if the gates of heaven rolled open, and we were all sitting in the throne room together, talking directly to God. I'd experienced such things before, just never in a staff meeting, especially at one where we were looking at the possibility of shutting down a ministry.

When my friend finished praying, everyone remained silent. I can't imagine what anyone might have added. Nor could I imagine that God might be ready to put an end to the ministry this servant of His had begun. It didn't make sense. But I couldn't argue with the numbers.

Then my friend shocked everyone. He was a very thin man, with long fingers that had once played concert piano. He lifted one of those bony fingers in the air and pointed at each of us, one by one, as he said, "Fifty years ago, God called me into ministry and told me to do one thing—be a soulwinner. I don't know what we're going to do about money, but I know that I'm going to be found faithful to that calling.

"So, here is the plan. We're going to go on the biggest soul-winning march this ministry has ever seen. For the next forty days, I want everything we do and every penny we spend to be a direct effort to win lost people to Christ. We're going to invite all my pastor friends from the area to bring their congregations and to ask their congregants to bring their unsaved friends. I'm going to call every pro athlete and celebrity I know, and we're going to witness to these people—without taking an offering. Get on the phones. Let's get some folks saved."

His statement was met with shocked silence, until his faithful assistant finally spoke up. "I have a list of about a hundred area churches," she said. "We could divide it up and start making calls."

The operations officer was next to speak. "I can put the phones on auto-answer for all incoming calls so that the lines will be free for making calls out."

"I'll write a script real quick," said the marketing director, "so we're all on the same page."

"Whenever someone gets a pastor on the phone, have the call transferred to me," said the events director.

The very next day, one local church called all its members and asked them to invite their unsaved friends to a special "evening of love" at the ministry. A about a quarter of the congregation agreed to do just that. By the following day, two more churches had joined in the effort. A stream of famous personalities came into town to promote the event. No offerings were ever taken, and nothing more was said among the staff about the needed money. They were too busy managing the sudden revival.

There is no way to profit financially from soul-winning outreach. The metrics are upside down, because soul-winning efforts target those who have yet to surrender to Jesus—usually, people with no incentive to support evangelistic outreach. Even unsaved people will give generously to feed the hungry, house the homeless, and set the captives free; but, for some reason, even believers don't support evangelism—especially local outreach efforts—with the same generosity and commitment.

Nobody would consider ministry a money-making enterprise, first and foremost. In that sense, the church is required to trust God for its income. I think it is God's way of collectively building the church's faith and trust in Him. In God's economy, when we seek Him first, everything follows. (See Matthew 6:33.) When we prioritize evangelism and ministry, the money we need will follow, as we act in accordance with the purposes of God.

My friend spent every dime he had (and some dimes he didn't have) and preached roughly fifty times, holding multiple meetings on the weekends. And then, forty days to the minute after he had announced that he would be found faithful, a businessman no one knew wrote a check to the ministry. The amount was just enough to start turning things around. Finally, there was something I could do! I helped them reorganize a bit to ensure that their financial troubles wouldn't repeat themselves. They continued in ministry for another fifteen years, until the leader's wife passed away, at which point he retired.

In business, we work with numbers and math, with reality and surety. In faith, we do things in spite of those factors, because faith is the substance that creates reality. (See Hebrews 11:1.)

⌒

Minding His Business **Basic Principle:**

The vision is the leader's. When all else fails, pray! Then walk in obedience to whatever God says to do.

CHAPTER 21

RENDER UNTO CAESAR

When asked by His disciples whether it was right to pay the tax, Jesus told His followers to render unto Caesar what was Caesar's. (See Matthew 12:21; Mark 12:17.) Then, He Himself made provision for the disciples to pay the tax. When the disciples got the money, they *paid the tax*.

Churches and nonprofit organizations are not exempt from rending unto "Caesar" what is his by right. Nonprofits are exempt from some taxes, and churches are exempt from unemployment insurance and Cobra for labor law; but, when it comes to most of the laws of commerce, the church is not exempt.

When I take on a new church client, one of the first things I do is check to make sure that their IRS filings are current and complete. When you start a nonprofit, you have to incorporate in your state, appoint board members who are legally liable for the actions of the organization, and file a 1023 form with the IRS. Then you receive a determination letter from the IRS that officially classifies your organization as a 501(c)(3). After that, you have to file a Form 990 with the IRS every year. Failure to do so results in a forfeiture of your nonprofit status.

The second thing I usually do is check for inurement, or instances of inappropriately benefitting from the nonprofit status. I find that it's best if the principals of a nonprofit organization simply receive a salary—no allowances for a vehicle or for personal landscaping or other perks. Even though these activities may be legal and even ethical, most are taxable; and keeping track of all the transactions, and having to provide proof in case of an audit, is an enormous burden. Furthermore, the Bible tells us to give not even a hint of impropriety (see Ephesians 5:3), and to some people, these types of allowances are improper. Arguments over such things can be avoided if the principles just receive a salary.

Next, I usually check expense reports and credit card statements, because that's what an auditor would do. Why? Because this is the number one area where abuse and neglect occur. Please make it a policy to reimburse only the reported transactions that are accompanied by a receipt. If your credit card statement says you spent $500 at Walmart, and you don't have a receipt, the IRS auditor may wonder if you purchased a new television for your house rather than supplies essential to your ministry. Reimbursements are legitimate only if substantiated by a receipt that proves the money was spent on materials pertaining to the exempted purpose of the organization.

One of the biggest areas of confusion and abuse is the purchase of meals. An employee of a nonprofit organization is not to expect reimbursement for a lunch just because he spent it talking business with his colleagues. A church should cover the meal of a staff member only if it required him or her to come in early or stay late. There must be a bona fide business reason or expectation of gain. The church may pay for a parishioner to dine with an employee or a special guest; but, again, there must be a bona fide business reason or expectation of gain. I know that ministry employees buy each other's meals all the time. Many people believe this to be an acceptable business practice. If you are among them, please look up "de minimis meals" on the IRS Web site, then swallow hard, thank God you have not been audited, and stop doing it.

When you serve a meal on the premises—say, for a staff meeting—the de minimis rule comes into play. It allows you to offer nominal benefits to your employees, such as personal use of the photocopier; snacks; event tickets; holiday gifts; and reimbursement for meals, transportation, and cell phone bills related to overtime work. In other words, you can get away with offering these kinds of benefits, but only rarely—not as a general rule.

Other than these occasional exceptions, everything an employee of a nonprofit receives from his employer is considered to be taxable income. Treating non-wage benefits as anything other than income is an infraction that the government remedies by collecting the back tax, then levying fines and penalties, starting with the employee who didn't claim the lunch or the photocopies as income on his tax return.

Another area I check closely is revenue. For example, if a church rents out its facilities for a "non-sacred event," such as a basketball game, the church is receiving income unrelated to the exempted purpose of the organization—income that is therefore taxable. This kind of revenue is called unrelated business income by the IRS, and it is taxable. Now, some clever pastor may argue that the gymnasium is being used for outreach. But he needs to make that argument with the support of an accountant and/or a lawyer, and he needs to hope he wins. If your building is rented for anything other than the purposes that qualify you as a nonprofit, it's taxable. Returning to our example of renting out a gymnasium, the back taxes can add up to thousands of dollars. Failure to pay could result in your having to pay the tax plus penalties and interest, which could easily double or even triple the tax you owed in the first place.

Along the same lines, nonprofits and churches are not exempt from copyright law—or the consequences of infringement. You cannot broadcast music that is not in the public domain without paying royalties to the writers and the production companies. Whether it's a song lyric, a movie line, an excerpt from a television show, or another type of media, make sure you pay for the rights to use it, if necessary. The kindhearted, loving worship artist whose music you adore may not care, one way or the other; but there are plenty of third-party firms that search the Internet every day, trying to catch instances of copyright infringement to report to the record label, for example, in hopes of getting part of the proceeds of the royalties, along with interest, fines, and legal costs.

If you are a pastor or another type of ministry leader, please don't ask an employee to wash your car, clean your house, cut your lawn, watch your kids, walk your dog, schedule you a haircut, or do any other personal service on company time. If you do, you should pay him or her out of your own pocket. And don't try using the excuse, "He was just volunteering, as a faithful church member." While it's perfectly fine for a church member to come to your house and voluntarily cut your lawn, a ministry employee, even one who attends your church for worship, is a different matter. Even if the employee wants to provide the service, the burden, as well as the penalties, rests with the employer to follow federal wage and hour laws.

Any employees who attend your church and desire to volunteer there must do so in a capacity that is unrelated to their salaried job. For example, your church's accountant can legitimately volunteer by singing in the choir, babysitting children in the nursery, or doing the landscaping; just don't have him count the offering, register guests, record data, or do any other voluntary task that is administrative in nature. Otherwise, the Wage and Hour Division of the U.S. Department of Labor will view his volunteering as work for which he should be paid according to federal regulations.

Here's another thing to keep in mind. If you require your employees to attend worship services there as a condition of employment, the time they spend at the church on Sundays is considered work. So, if an employee spends forty hours working during the week and two hours attending church on Sunday, you are obligated to pay him for two hours of overtime. It takes only one employee, past or present, to report the church to the proper federal agency, and you will find yourself owing overtime pay, interest, and penalties to every employee, past and present, for up to the last seven years.

Finally, a word to pastors and ministry principals: What you don't know *can* and *will* hurt you. Whenever the infringement of federal regulations and legal requirements makes it to the light of day, someone usually has to pay. Through the years, I have seen enough of these matters result in legal proceedings to know that ignorance is not a valid defense.

But don't take my word for it. Ask your lawyer or your accountant. And please don't shoot the messenger.

⌁

Minding His Business Basic Principle:

*Protect yourself and your ministry by paying your taxes,
filing reports, paying fees, and engaging someone who
knows what you should know, but don't know.*

CHAPTER 22

MINISTRY IS IN THE MARGIN

An early televangelist coined the phrase "Souls don't sell." Anytime I quote him, people look at me like I'm some sort of evil pagan. But the truth is, it's very hard to raise money to win souls for the kingdom. It's difficult to convince people to give money to send someplace they've never heard of to reach other people they'll never meet, especially if the people being asked are recent converts. Churches and evangelistic ministries need to generate cash surpluses on their operations if they expect to fulfill their purpose. It's a cold, hard truth: Church members the world over do not give enough money to send every soul to heaven.

Now, I'm terribly sorry if I'm the first one to break this news to you. But if you know the Scriptures, Jesus said it, too, when He told His disciples that the poor would always be among them. (See Matthew 26:11; Mark 14:7; John 12:8.) The truth is, most poor people are never going to earn enough money, on their own, to get out of poverty. It's possible but not likely. They need help. Most hungry people are never going to raise enough money to get fed. And no unsaved people are going to visit an evangelistic meeting of their own volition, much less throw enough coins into the offering to cover the cost of the meeting. The money to help both groups must come from another source.

A Protestant minister I know used to travel the globe between Sundays, holding meetings to win people to Christ. I was on his ministry's mailing list, and they were always asking for money. I did some investigating and discovered they had a budget of $15 million. Every penny they had, they poured into these evangelistic meetings held all over the world.

One year, they received decision cards from just over 42,000 people. I did the math: They had one person come to Christ for every $350 they received in donations. That figure may not mean much, but let's compare it with the same statistic from another church I worked with.

This church was located on a busy street in an affluent neighborhood. They had a stunning cathedral-style sanctuary with an impressive pipe organ. Regular attendees numbered about 2,000, and the annual budget was $3 million. In any given year, they might have had a hundred people come to know Christ through their services. Thus, they spent $30,000 per convert. Compare that to three hundred fifty dollars per convert.

How can one church spend so little money and still win so many to the cause of Christ, while another spends so much and wins so few? One church was investing its margin in evangelism; the other was paying for hand-carved pews, routinely steamed carpets, and frequent washes of the stained-glass windows. Both churches were spending their money on people—the first, on the lost; the second, on the saints who regularly attended.

We can't afford to content ourselves with raising just enough money to meet the needs of our own budget. If the church is going to make a difference in the world, it needs to bring in more money than it spends on itself. Margin, surplus, or profit—whatever name we call it, we need to make a return on our investment.

Many churches have a negative attitude toward profits, espousing the belief that the church should not be concerned about making money and that planning for profits is somehow greedy. They think that business-minded people cannot possibly be concerned about the things of God. But making a profit does not necessarily present an ethical or a moral conundrum. Making money is not ungodly, though it may be gained by ungodly means. Having money is not immoral, though it may be spent on immoral things. It's what you do with the surplus that determines the moral and ethical value. Which is more moral: the church that always asks for money but spends most of what it makes on missions and evangelism, or the church that never asks for money but spends most what it makes on itself, in the form of programs and facilities?

Terms like "margin" and "return on investment" make some people squirm, especially in churches that view profits as evil. But such a view is illogical. Which is better: to have some money left over at the end of the year, or to continuously spend more than you take in?

I've heard people say of me, "He's all about the money." As if ensuring one's bank account is necessarily an indication of greed! To me, it's not an issue of greed but of stewardship. If you don't talk about business, you won't make the money needed to advance the cause of Christ.

A church brought on a new pastor with a strong business background. He turned the regular staff meetings into discussions about how better to manage the business of the church. Whenever a staff member or volunteer would present him with an idea, he would ask, "What is the projected return on investment?" He put a lot of energy toward managing the church's business.

Departing from the tradition of preaching on stewardship only once a year, the pastor started asking for money fairly frequently. The parishioners started to complain, saying, "All he thinks about is money." As it turned out, all he thought about were souls. After about a year, he was ready. He had been preparing to launch a major evangelistic outreach, and he'd had enough wisdom to realize that it wouldn't break even. So, he had filled his war chest before going to battle for souls in his new city.

When it comes to the church, it's the job of the businessperson to create margin whenever and wherever possible so that there will be a surplus. This aim is not unethical. Trying to create the largest surplus in the history of your organization is a good goal. It's what you decide to do with that surplus that determines the ethics of it. Many ministries, especially those operating overseas, are doing great work; they simply cannot get enough funds. If your church brings in a surplus, you have the option of helping these ministries instead of spending everything on your own congregation.

Managing church business well enables us to generate a surplus, which empowers us to do the greatest amount of good. A church or ministry surplus that's earmarked to fund the vision of the pastors God has called to lead His kingdom is a great thing to have. There should always be surplus in the church. But you have to plan for it, manage it, and ask for it. And the more you do of each, the more surplus you will have.

⌒

Minding His Business Basic Principle:

Having a surplus in your church isn't immoral; it's the way you spend your church's money that determines the morality and ethics of it.

CHAPTER 23

HOW TO CREATE MARGIN

A church was sending two hundred people to help with the relief efforts after a hurricane in a city four hundred miles away. Historically, those participating in church-sponsored domestic mission trips had always traveled by caravan, with various members offering to drive. This time, however, it was decided that they should charter several tour buses.

"Why use buses?" I asked during a meeting.

"Some people don't want to drive their own cars," several people replied.

I am always suspicious when a few people speak for everyone.

"Name them," I said.

"That's the feedback we're getting," one offered.

"From whom?" I asked.

I never got an answer to that question. I rarely do.

The meeting concluded, but my investigation was just getting started. As it turned out, one minister's car was in the shop. It came as no surprise to discover that the minister with the broken-down car was the very person who'd suggested chartering buses. Of course, nobody had wanted to argue with him.

In the end, we canceled the contract with the bus company and found plenty of people who were thrilled to drive their own cars. Why? Because we'd told them how much money we would save—and how we planned to use it instead. Using the margin we created by canceling the buses, we filled a 24-foot U-Haul truck with emergency relief supplies to help the hurricane victims. This example is the perfect model of how business should be conducted by the church in order to create and spend margin.

If an undertaking is meant to create margin, someone at the table has to talk about such practical considerations as price, cost, and return on investment. A committee will tell you, "These are a must-have." "This is a have-to." The voice of business wants to cut the "must-haves" and "have-tos" in order to create the margin that will enable the church to serve as many people as possible.

There is always a tension between vision and practicality, but both are necessary. Even the pastor who wants to keep his church broke—the pastor who keeps his members dreaming of things so big, they could never happen unless God showed up—has to take practical steps toward that which he is trying to accomplish. The voice of business should not argue with the faith of the visionary, and the visionary might not follow the voice of business with exact precision; but they should honor each other.

When yours is the voice of business at the table, you'll probably often find yourself all alone, up against the masses. Such a solitary position will inevitably wear on you. But a nonprofit that plans on operating within its means learns to honor the voice of business and the practical issues it raises.

Being the voice of business is tough. I like to compare the task of managing church business to herding butterflies. A lot of sound business minds refuse to work with churches and other nonprofits because it can be hard, frustrating work.

In the last several decades, the perspective on work in the church, has changed. Thirty years ago, if you worked for a church or a charity that was run largely by volunteers, you were thankful if you got a paycheck. People expected to work long, hard hours for low pay, but they were passionate about the cause and thankful to be paid *anything* for helping to make a difference in the world.

What was once a calling has, for many, now become a profession. Many ministry staff who work forty-one hours want "comp time" for that extra hour. There are labor laws to be followed, of course, and no one should be abused; but, by and large, when a ministry employee demands comp time, then it's time to stop paying people to stand in each other's office doorways, sipping coffee while talking about nothing, instead of spending their time productively to move the mission forward.

A church was organizing a youth event that quickly ballooned to a huge investment. It started with a simple idea to give every kid a free T-shirt. Soon, they were giving them all shorts, too. For $40 each, they were giving away uniforms—to teenagers! The pastor called me in to help run interference with the youth pastor. From experience, I knew that a youth pastor with a bright idea is like a terrier with a bone—he doesn't want to let it go. I knew what I would have to do.

"You're not getting shorts and T-shirts," I told the youth pastor bluntly.

He grumbled about how I didn't love God because now the kids weren't going to look cool.

"With a thousand kids participating, at forty dollars each, that's forty thousand dollars," I told him.

"It's not about the money," he said.

Understand this: People who say, "It's not about *the* money," really mean, "*Your* money isn't the issue." They would never spend *their* money on it.

I started down a path of reasoning. "Good," I said. "Then we'll cut your pay in half, and that will cover part of it."

"No!"

"You're spending forty dollars per person. Are you charging forty dollars per person?" I asked.

"Yes."

"And that's going to pay for the lighting and the band and the amplification, right?"

"What's your problem?" he asked.

He hadn't considered all the costs that would be entailed by the concert portion of the event. Instead of admitting his mistake, he started questioning my salvation. He really had good intentions; he just had zero financial finesse. He was a lover of people, not an accountant.

I ignored his retort, took out a pencil and a piece of paper, and started detailing the concert costs. I showed him that he would have to either raise the price of the event, get more people to come, and/or cut costs. He opted for the latter. Once we cut out the shorts and T-shirts, we were able to forecast a margin of $10,000 for the event.

I said, "Now, what do you want to do with the ten thousand dollars you just saved?"

He lit up. "We could do an outreach in the high schools!"

"Now you're talking," I said.

He could hardly believe I hadn't fought him on it.

He bounded out of the meeting, more excited than ever at all the good that was going to come after the youth event.

The interesting end to that story is that one young man who received Christ during the outreach that resulted from the profits of that youth event became a friend of mine. He is serving as a youth pastor today, and all because we created some margin.

Minding His Business Basic Principle:

Money may follow ministry, but margin pays for it.

PART III:

MANPOWER

CHAPTER 24

YOU CAN TRAIN A DOG TO CLIMB A TREE

The pastor of a suburban congregation of about nine hundred people in an affluent community called me in to help with some member retention issues. The church's pastor of Christian education really stood out to me. I didn't work with him directly, but he was clearly a people person. Hospitable, handsome, well-educated, and well-liked, he always remembered everyone's name. I also noticed that in the time he'd been employed at the church—a little over a year—no new Bible studies had been offered. It wasn't my area, but I couldn't help wondering why.

"Where'd you find him?" I ventured to ask the pastor one day.

"He came from a church that had 50 percent of its congregants participating in a Bible study," the pastor answered.

"Wow, impressive," I replied. "I hope you'll have some new studies starting here soon."

"Well, he's still just getting to know the congregation. Still assessing things."

In my opinion, a one-year assessment was far too long, but I didn't say so then.

Talking with a few others, I found out that the pastor of Christian education had enlisted about forty people to help overhaul the church's education program. The participants often gathered at his house for cookouts or to watch a sporting event on television.

One afternoon, while the church staff was in a meeting, I decided to take a short break from my work and do some investigating. First, I checked on the pastor's Internet usage at the church and found that he'd been spending between fifteen and twenty hours a week blogging and/or writing blog posts for other ministries' Web pages.

Next, I called the church where he'd last worked—one he'd planted, in fact. The secretary had no qualms chatting about him. She really liked him, as everyone did. She told me that about half the congregation of 140 people used to go to his house twice a month for a barbeque. That was his idea of a Bible study.

"He was so fun to be with," she said. "It took us a while to unravel all the financial books after he left, though, because, as you may know, he was no administrator. He didn't like writing checks or filling out reports. And he really did not like deadlines. He just liked people!"

After our conversation, I approached the pastor of his current church and said, "This guy can sing and preach, and he's one of the most magnetic personalities I've ever met. But he left his previous church because he wasn't administrative enough to sit down and write checks. He didn't take care of business. And if he didn't take care of business when it was his money, what makes you think he is going to do so when it's your money? Oh, and the 'Bible studies' were really just barbeques at his house."

The pastor didn't lay him off; the man eventually left on his own, with nothing to show for his time at that church: no Bible studies, no revamped Sunday school lessons, no home groups. Last I heard, he had started a church in his hometown and was still blogging and writing for other ministries on the side.

Why? Because that was what he wanted to do all along!

Cats, squirrels, and monkeys all do a great job at climbing trees. But you can also train a dog to climb a tree. My friend can send her little Boston terrier right up a tree by saying, "Get the squirrel, Dixie!" But when my friend walks away, Dixie comes right back down. My friend has never walked into the backyard and found her dog in a tree. Why? Because even a dog that can climb a tree won't climb a tree unless it's told to. Climbing trees is simply not a natural act for a dog.

Cats climb trees because they can; they'll climb whatever they're able, it seems. Squirrels climb trees because that's where they live, as well as where they find their meals. Monkeys climb trees to get bananas, to sleep, or to escape a lion. If the job is to climb a tree, hire a squirrel. If you can't get a squirrel, hire a monkey or a cat. But never hire a dog. Even if a dog is capable of climbing trees, it isn't something most dogs want to do.

My point is that, left to their own devices, people will do what they want to do. It isn't a matter of honesty and integrity; it's just human nature. When you hire someone, you hire his nature—the way God has knit him together. So, it's smart to hire people who have the "want to," not just the "can do" or "will do" (or even the "have done"). Hire people who truly desire to fulfill the specific role for which you are hiring them.

And never hire someone just because he's a "good Christian." A creative, relationship-oriented person would make a lousy data analyst or accountant, regardless of his zeal for Christ; he's better off engaging with and inspiring people. Likewise, I probably wouldn't hire an accountant to lead praise and worship or a drill sergeant to teach kindergarten Sunday school.

I was once involved in a multibillion-dollar business that would buy out its competitors—mostly small "mom and pop" enterprises—and offer the business owners employment in our company. Most of them accepted our offer, but not for long. Having known what it is to be the number one decision maker in a company, they struggled to take orders from someone else, adhere to rigid policies, and endure annual performance appraisals. Every single one of them eventually remembered why he had started his own business in the first place and eventually left our company. All but one started another business as soon as they could do so without breaking their noncompete agreement. Why? Because someone who's been number one usually does not want to be number two. We should not have expected these naturally independent entrepreneurs to spend the rest of their working lives as employees rather than employers, as followers instead of leaders. It was not in their nature.

I have interviewed thousands of potential employees for every type of job you can think of—salespeople, skilled tradespeople, artists, musicians, singers, accountants, janitors, warehouse workers, executives, teachers, and pastors. One question I always ask is, "What do you *want?*" If you desire a straight answer about what people really want to do, ask them what they do even when they don't have to do it. Ask them what they do for fun. Ask them what they liked the best about their last job—and what they liked least—and why. Their answer will reflect their attitude toward outcomes and inputs (task-oriented), people, relationships or creative outlets (creative/relational).

The question "What do you want?" is bound to catch an interviewee off guard, because most people approach a job interview focused on what they think the interviewer wants. If, during the course of an interview, it seems that the candidate would want to do the things I need done, and would even enjoy doing them, I may end up hiring the wrong person if he was putting forth a persona based on what he believed I would want. When this happens, people end up with jobs they either can't do or don't want to do. It is a recipe for low productivity, high turnover, and low morale.

The most effective employees are those whose assigned responsibilities are things they truly love to do. Yet hiring people to do jobs they are not wired to do is a mistake I've watched church leaders make again and again. I can't tell you how many times I've seen churches hire really nice, creative, relational individuals who love God and love people, and give them jobs that are task-oriented and systems-driven. Asking a people lover to do data input and record-keeping is like asking a dog to climb a tree. The dog will do it, but it won't stay in the tree very long on its own. It's not a natural act.

~

Minding His Business Basic Principle:

Remember that when you hire people, you hire their nature and their character. It's wise to find out what people want to do, then give them a job doing it.

CHAPTER 25

WINNERS WANT TO KEEP SCORE

Do you measure performance by how well-liked a person is or by the results he produces? Do you measure performance at all? Top performers generate results that can be measured. Most churches suffer from a lack of accountability. Like it or not, inspection is the genesis of measurement, and measurement is the foundation of accountability. And accountability is the catalyst for sustained results.

My three sons, now adults, grew up as year-round athletes. My wife and I spent almost twenty years either sitting in hot, smelly gyms or standing on cold, rainy sidelines. The school district's athletic department wasn't particularly strict about tryouts. If a kid wanted to play a sport, he could—at least at the junior varsity level. But at the varsity level, only the best players were put in the game. Eventually, some parents started showing up at school board meetings, complaining that they didn't want to continue paying the athletic department fees if their children weren't going to be allowed to play. In their mind, equal opportunity to play was more important than winning.

I remember a particular meeting at which one mother argued this point with great intensity. She concluded, "After all, winning doesn't matter. It's how you play the game."

Then, the star of the football team stood up. "If winning doesn't matter, then why do we have a scoreboard?"

The purpose of a score (measurement) is to recognize desired behavior (or a lack thereof) and to determine the winner (define success). Elite athletes want to live in a world where scores matter. Top performers want to work in an environment where results matter and where people are rewarded for making a positive contribution. If your church can't attract and retain top performers on its staff, if your church does a great deal of talk but has little to show for it, maybe you need to take a look at the work environment. Does your team spend most of its time worrying about what might go wrong or who might get upset? Or does your team spend its time making plans with the expectation of success and learning from its mistakes?

The problem with hiring top performers is that they always have other options, so you have to work hard to make your organization attractive to them. People who are good at what they do get to choose where they work. Top-performing businesspeople aren't happy working in organizations that lack accountability and fail to follow through with their plans. Top performers want a "scoreboard." They won't put up with chaos forever, and the truth is, they don't have to.

If you want to turn chaos into order, if you want to turn talk into results, maybe you should ask a top-performing manager or businessperson how he does it. I guarantee you that his response will include such words as "accountability," "consequences," "outcomes," and "inspection."

Top-performing people expect inspection and even invite it. Yet inspection is grossly missing from the church. For whatever reason, many church leaders feel obligated to trust every employee, no questions asked. They believe that asking questions or requiring verification is a disrespectful practice bound to offend the other party.

It works like this: A church almost always starts with creative, relational people who tend to hire other creative, relational people. As a group, when they finally hire an administrator to handle the things they can't do or don't want to do, the first thing they wonder is, *Will this person fit in?* During the interview, they don't often probe for nature and character. They might think, *Has this person ever done such-and-such?* but they also might accept any answer. Rarely have I found a church that asks the hard questions, does due diligence, makes the necessary phone calls, and ensures they aren't wasting money on personnel.

I once worked with a church that brought in a new pastor because the staff believed he would take them to the proverbial "next level." The guy was sharp, handsome, magnetic, and well-spoken; everyone loved him. Two years later, they were still talking about the original "new ideas," and they had added a lot of "really new ideas," but very little had been accomplished. They hired a bunch of new people and paid them big salaries and talked some more.

Soon, the church was racking up huge losses every month and had burned through almost all its cash reserves. The chair of the church board was an old friend of mine, and he asked if I would come in and help find a solution to prevent further losses.

At my very first meeting with their pastor, he told me how much he loved me and wanted to be my friend. He talked about his big vision and his great staff. He talked about how they had budgeted a 30-percent increase in attendance and giving. He talked and talked and talked and talked.

When he finally paused to take a breath, I asked, "How do you plan on attaining this growth, and what is your plan if you don't?"

He answered, "Anything you need—anything at all—you let me know."

Talk about avoiding the question.

"How?" and "What?" along with "Who?" "Where?" "When?" and "How much?" are the language of results. Doers answer those questions directly. Talkers don't.

I rolled up my sleeves and got to work. One day, as I was reviewing the church's payroll and personnel, I realized that the church had failed to uphold one of its own policies by neglecting to run a background check on the pastor before they hired him. The next day, I got a call from my friend on the church board, informing me that the pastor was offended by my request for a background check, and that I would no longer be needed.

Shortly thereafter, I met my friend for coffee.

"What kind of a person complains about a background check?" I asked him.

"What can I say? The board is enamored of this guy." He kept his eyes on the ground as he answered.

It took me a few days to gather my things and leave. I knew I was overstepping my bounds, but I ordered the background check anyway and paid for it out of my own pocket. Just as I was about to turn off the lights on my last day at the church, the results showed up. They were frightening. All I can safely say is that this guy was a mess.

The board didn't listen then, but they were forced to listen later, when a huge scandal broke. The local newspapers reported on it for months. Needless to say, that pastor is no longer employed by that church. Even so, the church is a mere shadow of the thriving congregation it once was.

Top performers want the score kept. Poor performers don't.

I was helping at another church where the pastor asked me if, on the side, if I would advise one of his ministers who had a lot of ideas but not a lot of organizational ability. I called a meeting with the minister and his wife, who acted as his assistant. At the end of the meeting, I sent them both an e-mail recapping our discussion and reminding them of the action items they had said they'd take care of.

I received a call from the minister. He was livid. "I've never been so offended!" the minister shouted. "You assigned tasks to my wife and me. You're not my boss!"

I told the pastor that I was sorry, but I wouldn't be able to help that particular minister.

They didn't keep him on staff much longer. It turns out that my feedback only confirmed what the pastor had already noticed: that this particular minister did not know how to follow through. Any type of structure made him uncomfortable because he viewed it as rigidity.

But even a stopped watch is right twice a day. Every now and then, a group in chaos will attract a top performer—someone who really gets the job done. If that top performer has to deal with late meetings, unmet deadlines, and unreturned e-mails or phone calls, he is likely to interpret such treatment as disrespect and may decide to seek employment elsewhere.

A well-known church in the Bible belt had a minister of biblical studies we'll call Bill. Bill was highly educated, but wasn't the nicest guy in the world. He had a reputation for being a real taskmaster. And he would admit to having a good bit of old-fashioned rigidity. He once spent eighteen months teaching a class on the book of 1 Peter. Some of the other ministers at the church didn't like working with him, but participation in adult Sunday school had increased from 20 percent of the congregation to 60 percent since he came on board, so they couldn't exactly complain.

Bill spent a lot of time in the pastor's office, hearing about how others on the team did not enjoy working with him. He tried his best to get along with the other staff members; but, no matter what he did, there were always a few people who would complain and nitpick the job he was doing. According to them, everything Bill did was wrong and "old school." The truth was, Bill was so productive, he made others on the staff look bad by comparison, thereby jeopardizing their cushy jobs.

Eventually, the pastor had heard enough grumbling about Bill. He put the "head complainer" in charge of the church's biblical studies program, figuring that he must know the right thing to do, if he was sure that what Bill was doing was wrong. A few weeks later, Bill resigned.

The guy who took over for Bill—we'll call him Brandon—was a hip, millennial kind of guy with phenomenal stage presence. His title was pastor of adult discipleship.

Brandon talked endlessly about what he was "going to do." When half the Sunday school classes completed their curriculum, he disbanded them, saying that the church was going to start discipling adults through home groups. But no home groups started up. Whenever a teacher of one of the few remaining classes would resign, he'd replace that person with a friend of his who may or may not have understood Scripture. And anytime a theological problem came up that the teacher was not equipped to address, Brandon never followed up on the inquiry.

Eventually, the pastor confronted Brandon. "You've been talking about home groups, but on what date will we have even one assembled? When is someone going to get on the phone and call people to ask, 'Would you like to be in a home group?'"

Insulted, Brandon flipped out. Then he went to both the church board and the denominational oversight committee to complain about the pastor's "unprofessionalism" and "lack of trust."

Over the next eighteen months, participation in adult Sunday school dropped from 60 percent to 5 percent. Then Brandon left the church.

Bill, a top performer, resigned from his position because he did not want to work in an environment where results were not respected and poor performers were not held accountable for their behavior and their lack of results. Brandon, a poor performer, resigned because someone dared to hold him accountable for his shortcomings. When poor performers go unpunished for their mediocre contributions and their failure to deliver results, top performers feel unappreciated and disrespected, and they're often compelled to move on, usually to a better job. They do this easily because they always have options. Poor performers, on the other hand, feel threatened by inspections and accountability, and they react by striking back. They have to fight, for they have few other options, if any.

If your team is not as productive as you expect them to be, it's probably time to increase your inspection and accountability. If there is a lack of inspection, it's likely because inspection involves hard, time-consuming work that is probably going to ruffle some feathers, and you're afraid of either the work or offending others. The same is true for accountability: it requires rewarding good performance (that's the easy part) and penalizing poor performance (that's the part everyone dreads).

If this discussion of inspection and accountability brings to mind the names of specific staff members who are lacking in these areas, it means that you've already identified the problem and are allowing yourself the luxury of avoiding having to deal with it. The lack of top performers on your team is a predictable byproduct of that luxury you're indulging. If that's the case, then once again, the church has sacrificed the eternal mission for temporary peace. Come on. You don't want that.

$\backsim$

Minding His Business Basic Principle:

Top performers expect inspection, and they thrive in environments where people are held accountable for the quality of their work.

CHAPTER 26

MANAGE OBSERVABLE BEHAVIORS

W hat you do speaks so loudly that I can't hear what you say," wrote Emerson. This is one of my favorite sayings, and it's also one of the key ethos through which I filter my life experiences. When a person's words and deeds don't match, *the truth is always in the deeds.*

You are really three different versions of yourself: the person you know yourself to be, the person you let others see, and the person other people really see when they look at you. If you want to see a person for who he really is, listen to what he says, then watch what he does, especially when he thinks no one is looking. The difference between what a person does and what he says is the most accurate indication of who he really is.

Years ago, a friend of mine had to undergo a medical procedure that would require him to take off work for several months to recover, and he asked me to fill in for him as the administrative pastor of a large church in Louisiana. My first day on the job, the pastor called a meeting to introduce me to the rest of the staff. He told them that I would be the "sheriff" while my friend recovered.

During the meeting, a young associate pastor I'll call Tom introduced himself, then told me matter-of-factly that he was a rule follower who believed in submission to authority. As he spoke, however, I couldn't help but notice how many people in the room rolled their eyes.

Soon after, I called the nice lady who kept the books, and asked to see the records of accounts payable.

"Including the credit card statements?" she wanted to know.

"Sure," I said. "Bring it all—everything you've got."

After she put the files on my desk, I noticed that there were three folders: one for payables, one for credit cards, and one labeled "Tom." The payables file and the credit card file were both relatively thin and well-kept. The file labeled "Tom" was thick and bulging with paper. As I dug into the first two folders, I quickly saw that the church paid its bills on time, and all was in order.

Tom's file was a different story. It was packed with endless communications from Tom demanding that a check be cut "right away," and correspondence from the accounting department requesting receipts, documentation, and expense reports from Tom.

I took the three files to Tom's office for some "fellowship."

"Tom," I said, "it looks like you owe the accounting department some paperwork."

"Do I?" he replied.

"Well, yes. If you look at this file, it seems like there is quite a bit of documentation lacking for a long time. When can we expect the documents requested?"

Tom's face was getting red. "I don't know."

"The rules say you need to provide this documentation within ten days. I thought you were a rule follower."

"I am," Tom replied. "When the rules aren't stupid."

"But this is the way the pastor wants his staff to conduct business."

Tom's response was clear: "Well, Pastor does not always get what he wants."

Clearly, Tom's words (the Tom he wanted me to see) did not match Tom's deeds (the Tom I saw). The difference between his words and his deeds, combined with the reaction of his coworkers when we first met, indicated to me that, contrary to his statement, Tom was not, in fact, a rule follower; he was rebellious and probably not dependable (the Tom he probably knew himself to be).

My friend recovered and returned to work before I got any paperwork from Tom. Tom no longer works at that church.

I was called in to help another church, this one in Canada. It was too long of a flight for my comfort requirements, but the fishing there was great, and I'll tell you later how I know that. This church was trying to solve a number of problems, primarily how to attract enough members to volunteer. They had hired a kindly retiree to do volunteer recruitment. He had spent a lifetime running a press in a manufacturing facility. I wondered how that qualified him to recruit volunteers.

My first step was sitting down with him and asking why the volunteer sign-up sheet for every project was blank.

"No one wants to volunteer," he said.

"How do you know?"

"No one is volunteering."

"How many people have spoken these words to you: 'I don't want to volunteer'?"

"Not many."

"How many people have you spoken to?" I asked him.

"I make fifty calls per week," he said.

"How many people have you spoken with this last week?"

"I think I reached two, and they said they'd get back with me," he said.

This man's behavior indicated that he was willing to recruit volunteers but really did not want to and certainly did not know how. The problem was, he was making calls but not actually speaking to anyone. And on the rare occasion that he connected with someone, he never followed up with him. His definition of "success" was dialing fifty phone numbers, not speaking with fifty people. He often made his calls during the day, when most of the congregation was at work. People don't always answer their phones, and they return voice mail messages even less frequently. Success required that he connect with fifty people, not just dial their numbers. I could almost imagine the man dialing, getting a recording, and thinking, *Thank God!* He just wasn't the right fit for the job.

We can manage only the behaviors we observe. Someone who really wanted to recruit a lot of volunteers would try a host of different tactics until he found one that proved successful. Anyone who has successfully recruited volunteers knows that you have to ask one person at a time. You have to make calls in the evenings and on weekends. You have to ask people in person at church. You have to *contact* people, not just call them. And contacting people often requires multiple phone calls. The rule of thumb, by the way, is that if you dial ten people five times each, you'll speak to eight of them once. A great recruiter doesn't rely solely on passive techniques like e-mails and sign-up sheets. These techniques are rarely as effective as a friendly people-lover asking one potential volunteer at a time. That's the behavior of someone who knows how to recruit volunteers and wants to do so.

After my interview with the man in charge of volunteer recruitment, the pastor placed him in another position and promoted one of his assistants to the role of volunteer coordinator. In a day, the problem was solved. To celebrate, the pastor took me fishing.

At another church, there was a smiling, sweet, affectionate guy who had the brightest shock of red hair I'd ever seen. Maybe that's why people called him Red. Red was the worst volunteer at the church. He would sign up for the grounds work day, the charity walk, the set-up crew, and so forth, but he rarely showed up. Red was the butt of many jokes told by the staff.

When I caught wind of this "terrible" volunteer, I decided to observe him for a while. It didn't take me long to realize that Red was a people lover. On Sunday mornings, you could see (and hear) his enthusiasm as he greeted and hugged person after person. It seemed Red knew everybody in the church. To Red, a stranger was just a friend he had yet to meet.

I called the volunteer coordinator. "If you need to have people greeted, if you need to manage the pastor's meet-and-greet, or if you need to reach fifty people by phone, Red's your guy," I told her.

"He never shows up," she said.

"He never shows up to do what he doesn't like doing—painting, walking, setting up chairs. The only reason he signs up is because he wants to be with the *people* who signed up."

The volunteer coordinator followed my recommendation, and soon Red became an indispensable part of the ministry team. When he made calls, he punched numbers like mad until he finally got to talk to someone. Then he was ecstatic. He could work a room better than any politician. It was very hard not to smile when you were with Red. When the volunteer coordinator shifted the tasks and made him her ally, he scored a home run every time.

Remember to believe what you see, not what you hear. Someone who insists that he loves people may not be very loving when you have to correct his behavior. "Loving people" might be code for "Loves being approved by others." Someone who claims to be a planner needs to have results for his planning. Without results, he's really just a person who likes structure or has high control needs.

Results are the byproducts of deeds. Talk is productive only insofar as one's words influence and inspire productive behavior. The reason we should manage observable behaviors is because nothing is accomplished until something is done. If you want to control outcomes, you must manage deeds.

~~~

Minding His Business **Basic Principle:**

Believe what you hear until proven wrong. Trust what you see. Manage deeds.

CHAPTER 27

STAY OUT OF HARM'S WAY, PART 2: EMPLOYMENT LAW

I'm not your lawyer or your CPA, but let's talk a little about how to stay out of harm's way when it comes to overtime, compensatory ("comp") time, and performance reviews. One of the biggest mistakes I see in churches is making every employee "salaried" and believing that will exempt the church from having to pay them for overtime. The Wage and Hour Division (WHD) of the U.S. Department of Labor designates salaried employees as either classified or unclassified. Unclassified salaried employees are not eligible for overtime, but classified salaried employees are.

There are specific factors that qualify a salaried employee as "unclassified," and the most obvious is that an unclassified salaried employee spends at least 50 percent of his time supervising others directly and has the power to hire and fire. Certain creative employees, such as graphic artists, ministers, or Web site developers, whose work is creative and inspirational, can also be considered "unclassified." They can be salaried, but they won't receive pay for overtime. With a few other exceptions, any classified salaried employee must be paid overtime for any work that exceeds forty hours in a seven-day period.

One pastor's administrative assistant worked long hours and seemed to be constantly on call. I asked the accounting department to show me her time card, but they said she was "salaried" and didn't have to log her hours. They were mistaken. Just because she was salaried, it didn't mean she was "unclassified"; she still had to be paid overtime. I know that this might rock most pastors' worlds, but administrative assistants are not unclassified salaried employees. They must be paid overtime.

In this particular case, the pastor felt that the extra hours he demanded from his administrative assistant were indispensable. He often led services, made calls, and studied in the evening, and would require her assistance. She routinely worked more than forty hours a week but never received overtime pay. After all, she was "salaried."

I told the pastor he was asking for trouble. He was not happy with me, but he agreed to hire a student to come in at 4 p.m. each day to help the administrative assistant with filing and other tasks, so that her work week would not exceed forty hours.

The pastor tolerated the arrangement, but my engagement at that church was cut strangely short.

A year later, I was called back because the church was being audited by the WHD, with a specific inquiry into payroll and overtime. I helped the church provide the requisite records as the auditors turned their books inside-out and drilled down on every detail. When I had altered the schedule of the administrative assistant, my name had been mud to the pastor; but, by the end of the audit, some of the church administrators were naming their kids after me.

A number of times, I've had to clean up messes involving the volunteer work of paid staff members. In one church, the employees who staffed the day care during the week for pay also "volunteered" to work with children on Sunday mornings. This is not a legally viable arrangement, as we discussed in an earlier chapter. The day care workers would be eligible to sing in the choir or to serve on the usher team, but they can't volunteer to do a job similar to the one for which they receive a paycheck.

And, as we already established, if you require church attendance as a condition of employment or of continued employment, you have to count the attendance as work time. Anything you require of an employee in order for him to keep his job counts as a job function and, as such, is something for which he must receive pay. Furthermore, it is incumbent on the employer to enforce the regulation and, if need be, to discipline the "volunteering" employee for violating the workplace wage policy.

This brings us to the topic of compensatory time. If time off is given in exchange for overtime worked, it must be taken within the same pay period as it is earned. I learned this the hard way. I once ran a wholesale distribution business with both inside and outside salespeople working on straight commission. The compnay operated a multimillion-dollar call center. Many of the call center employees were single mothers who were often obligated to miss a day of work in order to take care of something related to their children. They appreciated that I allowed them to accumulate comp time so that they could meet their children's needs without having to take a day off.

You've likely heard the saying "Nice guys finish last," and in this case, it was true. What I learned was this: If an inside salesperson worked only thirty-five hours in a single pay period, and I paid her a full paycheck, the government saw my act as generous. But if that same individual worked 45 hours the following week, and that week belonged to the next pay period, then, regardless of what happened the week before, the government saw me as a cheat if I didn't pay her for overtime. That's how I found out that inside salespeople are classified differently than outside salespeople, and are eligible for overtime.

What happened next was heartbreaking.

An employee who was disgruntled about something else vented to a family member who was familiar with the compensatory time regulations established by the Wage and Hour Division (WHD) of the U.S. Department of Labor. The employee decided to file a complaint with the WHD, which conducted an audit of three years' worth of payroll records. They identified about a hundred employees who, over a three-year period, had earned about $35,000 in overtime pay for hours I had mistakenly identified as compensatory.

It gets worse.

I found out that an amount of $35,000, to the government, is actually $85,000. The smaller figure is what we should have paid the employees in overtime; the larger is what we had to pay, including interest and penalties. Furthermore, we had to attempt to contact every employee to whom we owed money; the burden was on me to find them all and to pay them their due. For all the people we could not locate, we had to put their money in a special bank account, then place an advertisement in the local newspaper twice a year, announcing that we still owed money to some of the people we had employed during the seven-year audit period. (How many people do you think called us falsely claiming to be one of the people to whom we owed money?) The unclaimed money remained in the bank account until it was eaten up by fees and the expenses of advertising its existence in hopes of finding the people to whom it belonged.

You can't make this stuff up.

There have been numerous high-profile lawsuits against church or ministry leaders calling on their staff to mow their yard, take their dog to the groomer, or perform other personal favors for no pay. I hope no one is doing that anymore. Every senior pastor should treat the mailbox at his house as if it were a time clock. If an employee walks past his mailbox, he's "on the clock" on the pastor's dime.

One more employee management challenge is worth mentioning, and that is personnel reviews with a raise attached to them. Unless your organization is large enough to afford a highly compensated human resources professional, I don't recommend tying raises or terminations to employees' performance reviews. Otherwise, it is difficult to ensure an objective standard of measuring performance. Behaviors that are tolerated in one department could get you fired in another. That is a lawsuit waiting to happen.

At the print firm I once ran, there were many jobs that required the printed pieces to be placed in envelopes. Being an inserter in the letter shop was a skilled position. After going through a lot of personnel troubles, I sat down with a journeyman who could insert 5,000 pieces per hour. We determined that a new employee should be able to start at 200 per hour and increase to 1,000 per hour within a month's time; otherwise, we would know that we hadn't hired the right person. Life became much easier when we fired sooner and promoted later.

In the church world, it is very difficult to quantify the measure of performance. There is a great diversity of responsibilities and skills. Because appraisals are largely subjective, and also because supervisors often wait until the last minute to do them, the reports should be evaluated by an objective party to ensure that everyone is held to the same standard. If you don't have a consistent standard of measuring performance, you make yourself vulnerable to a lawsuit, especially if the appraisals are tied to pay increases and promotions.

With the exceptions of some payroll exemptions for clergy, some unemployment regulations, and some HIPAA specifications, all the employment laws that apply to secular businesses apply to the church, as well. If you make a mistake, all it takes is just one employee who understands the law and knows where to lodge a complaint, or has a family member or a friend who will do it for him, and you will find yourself in a heap of trouble.

Now, a final word, to appease my lawyer: I'm not a lawyer. I am offering advice learned from personal experience. But please don't take my word for this. Call your own lawyer and your CPA for a consultation concerning such matters.

~

Minding His Business Basic Principle:

Get familiar with employment law, and pay someone whose profession it is to know the law and regulations to review your practices.

CHAPTER 28

DON'T BE A STATISTIC

You may have heard it said, "If it happens to one person, it's a tragedy; but if it happens to a million people, it's a statistic." Yet there is one personnel problem I've often seen that is itself a tragedy for every church it affects. That is, putting people in jobs they are not suited for, and not putting people in jobs that they *are* suited for. Sounds simple, right? Not always.

I worked with a very large urban church whose worship leader could sing the paint off the walls. Several thousand people showed up for the service every Sunday, most of them coming as much for the music as for the message. Not only was this man a magnetic worship leader; he was the consummate artist. He built a huge choir of faithful participants, arranged several vocal ensembles, coached soloists, and could do instrumentation off the top of his head. Furthermore, on Sunday mornings, he rocked the house. His was a blessed congregation.

The church board wanted his compensation to reflect their appreciation, as well as to be enough to prevent him from accepting a position at another church that would pay him more. But they were stymied as to how to redraw the salary structure. Meanwhile, the executive pastor resigned, leaving the board to search for his replacement. As they considered the description of the ideal candidate—great with people, understands the ministry, works well with other pastors—someone said, "Why don't we promote the worship leader to this position?" He figured they could kill two birds with one stone: increase the worship leader's pay and cut the budget by eliminating a position.

In my experience, highly creative people—including musicians, artists, and many pastors—tend not to thrive in administrative positions, such as that of executive pastor (basically a managerial role).

In the preface, I referred to the saying that goes, "No job is too hard for the guy who doesn't have to do it." Nobody on the church board saw the error in placing a highly creative, relational person in a position requiring technical and administrative skills. The creative, relational people who tend to lead the church are often ill-suited for the pragmatic work of running the church. That job is best left in the hands of get-it-done people. Relational people often view those with the get-it-done attitude as petty and small-minded, while the latter group often views the former as irresponsible and self-centered. And both sides think that the other group has it easy.

I'm always telling the get-it-done people to be quiet. After all, the relational person's inability to do the details is what provides get-it-done people's job security. And after all, can the get-it-done people pack the auditorium week after week? Also, when the creative relational people who are saying the get-it-done folks need to lighten up, I'll ask them if they would like to manage the waterfall of detail and disappointment that is the daily job of the manager and administrator. The truth is each thinks the other guy has the easy job, but could never do it.

As expected, the worship leader took the position and the larger salary. Within months, he was miserable. He hated all the seemingly trivial details he had to keep track of. His organizational skills were limited to voices and musical instruments. The incredible harmony that the church had enjoyed during his time as the worship leader exclusively was irreparably ruined. It wasn't long before he did exactly what the board had feared and left that congregation to bless another church with his musical skills.

No organization, churches included, can afford to place people in positions for which they are ill-suited.

Another church that had shrunken from 1,000 to 500 worshippers hired someone whose former title had included the word "marketing" and made her their "director of communications." The first thing she did was turn the church's monthly newsletter into a quarterly magazine. At the end of the first year, she'd spent $35,000 to print and distribute the magazine four times to four hundred households. Besides being incredibly expensive, the publication didn't reflect the priorities of the church. It might include a four-page devotional, but it didn't report on the mission trip the youth group had taken to Guatemala. One issue featured an interview with the membership coordinator, but the outreach event at which more than fifty people had given their lives to Christ received no mention whatsoever.

The director of communications spent the bulk of her work time writing. According to my estimation, over half of her time was devoted to writing and editing the magazine, the weekly bulletin, and personal letters and e-mails. Now, I'm not knocking writers. Writing is an important and often underappreciated skill. But this particular church needed a communications strategy, not a magazine.

The second thing the director of communications did was build a Web site that she then failed to maintain. The site got about a hundred hits per month, but it didn't even list the times of the Sunday services, and the monthly calendar was left blank. A site search for such terms as "children," "youth," "Bible study," "worship," and "service" yielded a single result: "No Data Found."

Third, the director of communication created an "electronic newsletter"—a PDF of the weekly bulletin that she e-mailed to about fifty snowbirds. Some strategy, huh?

When the church finally called me in to clean up the mess and give them a comprehensive communications strategy, I sat down with the director of communications and soon learned that her previous position had been that of a copywriter. She simply didn't have the credentials for the job they had hired her to do. Even worse, she did not recognize how woefully unqualified she was, so she fought me every step of the way. It was a difficult engagement.

Even so, we managed to launch a comprehensive communications strategy that included an updated Web site, a smartphone application, a Facebook page, and a weekly electronic newsletter. The Web site received thousands of hits per month. Furthermore, the quarterly magazine that had previously been sent to four hundred households was replaced by a weekly newsletter that went to over three thousand people. All these components cost less than the church had spent to produce the quarterly magazine alone, and, even better, they prompted immediate growth.

You simply cannot entrust a job to someone who isn't qualified to do it. This applies to yourself, as well, no matter how difficult it may be to own up to the fact of the matter.

A pastor called and asked me to help him figure out how to grow his church. He was a phenomenal leader who was well-beloved by his congregants, all of whom were growing spiritually because of his outstanding skills at the pulpit. When we met, I learned that his biggest concern was making sure that the congregation was aware of upcoming activities, like the youth car wash or the women's Bible study. He generally announced these events at the beginning of the worship service on Sunday, but the participation was less than desirable.

This "master communicator" could verbally deliver a message better than almost anyone else I had ever met, but that was the only way he knew to convey information. I pointed out that his announcements would be missed by anyone who arrived late to the service (and, of course, by those who didn't show up at all). He'd never thought of that.

He also hadn't thought about what might happen if the church advertised to the local community that an outstanding Bible teacher was in the house! He knew he could deliver, but all he could see was the too-short list of volunteers for the bake sale. When we took him off the communications team and started telling the community what they were missing if they didn't attend on Sundays, the church started growing.

~

Minding His Business Basic Principle:

Put people in jobs they're suited for, and don't give people positions they're not suited for. This goes for you, too.

CHAPTER 29

DON'T TOLERATE THE UNACCEPTABLE

In the church, strength of character is necessary for the tough personnel decisions that often need to be made in order to strengthen the entire church. Too often, a church keeps an employee on staff because it believes it's easier to tolerate his presence, however unhelpful, than to suffer the damage that will result from his dismissal. Most church leaders have probably made the choice to tolerate the negative behavior of a staff member in the short run rather than endure the wrath of the parishioners they believe will lament the staff member's departure in the long run. Unfortunately, these situations rarely get better with time. It's like a cancer patient who puts off surgery to remove a tumor because he fears the pain of the incision.

The best way to stay out of situations like this is to nip them in the bud. Don't believe me? I'll bet you'll believe Jesus, who said:

> *If your brother or sister sins against you, go and point out their fault, just between the two of you. If they listen to you, you have won them over. But if they will not listen, take one*

*or two others along, so that "every matter may be established
by the testimony of two or three witnesses." If they still refuse
to listen, tell it to the church; and if they refuse to listen even
to the church, treat them as you would a pagan or a tax collec-
tor.*   (Matthew 18:15–17)

Scripture is pretty clear: "If your brother or sister sins…, go….
If they do it again…, go and take some leaders with you…. If they
do it again, tell the church." Jesus did not say, "If your brother or
sister sins against you, just ignore it. If they do it again, just wait; it
will get better. And whatever you do, don't tell the congregation."
Yet how often we do just that! Can you think of one time when
tolerating unacceptable behavior made a situation better? I didn't
think so.

A large Southern church called me in to help balance the
budget and redirect funds in order to avoid losing money. They
had a longtime employee who had held many different positions
over the years. She hadn't proven herself exceptionally good at any
job, but she was well-beloved, and the pastor feared that her termination would upset too many members. For a while, she'd acted as
nursery director—and did a mediocre job. The rooms were always
chaotic and unkempt. Whenever parents would reunite with
their children after the Sunday service, they'd find them covered
in cookie crumbs and Kool-Aid stains. There were rarely enough
volunteers to care for even half the kids there. The nursery director wasn't a bad person; she had simply risen to her own level of
incompetency. But nobody wanted to tell her she needed to find
employment somewhere else, because doing so was bound to upset
"a lot of people."

So, as they had done again and again, the church leaders
assigned her a new job. This time, they made her the director of
worship arts. The first thing she did in her new position was order
a brand-new Apple computer for everyone involved in the worship
arts, as well as in Web development and audiovisual/graphic arts.

She said she wanted everyone working with the latest version of her favorite software, which evidently included many bells and whistles. Then, she ordered a Bose headset to go with each computer. No one stopped her.

As I was digging into the church's financials, I noticed a hemorrhage of cash in the department of worship arts. I asked a member of the accounting department for the donation records of some of the widows in the congregation, and then I scheduled a meeting with the director of worship arts.

"I need you to help me out with something," I told her.

"What's that?"

I showed her a list of ten widows in the congregation who lived on a fixed income. "I need you to call each of these ladies and tell her that she's going to have to tithe for the next twelve months in order to pay for the Bose headsets you bought for the members of your department. And, by the way, what does a graphic artist need a headset for?"

"I was thinking that it would make everyone happier and more productive," she replied, ignoring my first comment.

"Well then, call the ladies on this list."

She was ashamed in the moment, but she didn't get the message, because it wasn't long after this that she stalled a staff meeting with a discussion of which shade of teal would be appropriate for a drape over the Communion table.

I encouraged the church leaders to let her go, but they were still concerned that doing so would upset "a lot of people." They feared that her dismissal would cause the church to come across as cold, uncaring, and corporate.

On the contrary, the church had been extraordinarily generous and tolerant by retaining this employee of nominal skills and talents for so long, and letting her spend so much of their budget with so little to show for it. I suggested to them that if they wanted to honor her years of service, they could give her a sizeable severance package or let her use work time to search for a new position elsewhere. That way, they could tie their generosity in her time of termination to a separation agreement that would include a disclosure clause dictating her testimony and response regarding the separation. If the severance/separation package was generous enough, not only would the woman be likely to accept the terms, but if she complained about the church after receiving such generous treatment, she would seem ungrateful. Either way, the church would be in control of the message.

Resignations and dismissals are not necessarily negative. Often, when the church leaders try to correct an employee's behavior, the other staff will start to talk. You may hear a comment such as, "A lot of people really like her, and they might leave the church if we get rid of her." Whenever you hear someone make that type of statement, ask him the names of the "lot of people" in question, then identify from that list those who seem likeliest to leave. Every time I have walked the leadership staff of a church through this exercise, they have come to realize that "a lot of people" is never nearly as many as they originally thought. And, the truth is, some churches would probably be better off if a few of the "lot of people" did leave! Let's be honest—Jesus does not weep when someone stops attending First Baptist Church and switches to Calvary Baptist Church down the street. Let that pastor deal with him.

I consulted with a church whose associate pastor had been calling himself the "heir apparent" for the twenty-five years he had worked there. But when the senior pastor suddenly took ill and passed away, instead of promoting the "heir apparent," the church board conducted a search and hired someone else.

By this time, the "heir apparent" was sixty years of age. He felt worn-out and used, and soon became bitter and divisive. The leadership wouldn't fire him, lest "a lot of people" leave; but, because of his divisive behavior, many people *did* leave—and not necessarily the people the board had assumed would leave if he were fired.

This is an important concept to remember. It's a variation of "opportunity cost." While the retention of a low-performing church employee may not prompt many people to leave, the function of a low-performing employee is bound to prevent some first-time visitors from ever coming back. Longtime members aren't likely to pick up and leave just because the children's area is a mess, for example; but someone who's on the hunt for a new church home isn't likely to choose yours if something as "minor" as the state of the nursery fails to meet their expectations. Fewer people quit the church because the worship is lame than don't return for the same reason. Always remember to count the people who visited and didn't return when you think about the "lots of people" who might leave due to the dismissal of an ineffective church employee.

In this case, the new pastor did the math. When he realized how many people had left due to the attitude of the "heir apparent," he knew he couldn't afford to keep the man on staff. He took me out for a steak dinner to probe my brain about the situation. I told him, "He has to go. But, instead of a 'going,' make it a 'sending.' Give him enough money to make him happy, and send him to minister where his heart leads him. He has only five years left before the denomination will force him to retire, anyway."

The pastor went all-out, and the church named a hall after the man. They took up an offering for him, matched the amount, and then promised to keep in touch as he went to minister to indigenous people in a foreign nation, something he'd always wanted to do. They gave him a generous severance package, including a nondisclosure agreement, and named him "missionary in residence." The man couldn't have complained, even if he'd wanted to, because of the agreements he'd signed; but he didn't want to complain, because he felt respected. His years of service had paid off. The older church members felt good about it, and the new ones didn't really care whose name was on the hall where they met.

Here is a truth for all church leaders to keep in mind: No matter what you do or how well you do it, some people are going to leave at some point. Don't allow your desire to avoid the pain of "a lot of people" leaving to outweigh the wise decision to nip it in the bud. Your job is to be the voice of reason as you remind everyone, "We are here to put people in heaven. Those who don't see this vision of the church probably will never be pleased."

Remember, Jesus gave us a model for dealing with unacceptable behavior. Whether it is from a parishioner or a staff member, the steps are to (1) tell the person, (2) take some leaders along and tell the person again, and then (3) tell the whole church before "sending" the person on his way.

∿

Minding His Business Basic Principle:

Summon the strength of character to make the tough personnel decisions, no matter what "a lot of people" might do as a result. When you cut weaknesses, the whole church grows stronger.

CHAPTER 30

IF MONEY DIDN'T MATTER, WHOM WOULD YOU HIRE?

I grew up in central Ohio, where the Ohio State Buckeyes were the home team. One of the most revered coaches in OSU history was Woody Hayes, who had a well-known quote (at least in central Ohio): "You win with people." Hiring can and should be a crucial opportunity for growth in any organization. When a key employee vacates his post, and you're faced with finding a replacement, ask yourself the following questions: *What did I always find myself wishing he would do (differently)? Is there anything we are now free to do now that he's gone?* Once you have answered those questions, ask yourself one more: *If money didn't matter, whom would I hire?* You may be surprised how close you can get to finding the ideal candidate when your primary concern isn't finding one who will work for the same salary or less than the person he is replacing.

I was working with a large church in the Southwest to build its membership. Under the auspices of an outstanding director, the chancel choir had grown to an impressive size. They had robes, a pipe organ, an orchestra—the whole works. The director loved the dramatics of silently counting them down, then conducting them to sing the first chord full throttle. It was enough to blow your wig off. Theirs was truly one of the finest traditional church choirs I have ever heard.

The choir and its director alike were wildly popular with most of the parishioners. The only problem was, the congregation was aging and shrinking. As beautiful as traditional choir music is, you don't have to be an expert in church life to know that most of the congregations that are experiencing growth have some form of contemporary worship.

This particular choir director had no knack or desire for contemporary worship. He was old enough that people had begun to whisper about his retirement. But before any action could be taken, he contracted an illness that proved fatal. The pianist, who was also getting up there in years, was immediately promoted to choir director. It was a sudden and total disaster.

This wasn't my department, but I could tell that the pastor was preoccupied with worry about it. I suggested to him, "Instead of thinking about how to get a new choir director who will work for the same salary as the former one, let's ask ourselves, 'If we could have anything we wanted, what would praise and worship at this church look like? Would the seats be full? Would they be filled with young families praising God with hands raised and voices lifted up? Would there be special concerts? Guest artists? Multigenerational and multicultural services?' Then, let's ask, 'Who does that type of thing, and where would I find him?' At this point, let's not ask, 'How much will it cost?'"

It probably seems odd for a businessperson to suggest not worrying about the cost. That's because "opportunity cost"—the value of things that *don't* happen because of a course of action not taken—can be just as pricey. After suggesting that we think about what could be, I reminded the pastor to consider all the people who had not returned to the church after their first visit because, as talented as the chancel choir was, the selections they tended to sing were decreasing in popularity.

The pastor knew of a dynamic Dove and Grammy award-winning worship leader who was simply out of that church's league. But, just to get creative, the pastor called a meeting and threw out the man's name. One member of the leadership staff had a friend who knew him personally. After making a few phone calls, this leader was astonished to discover that the artist was open and available. What did not astonish him, however, was the man's expectation of a far higher salary than the previous choir director had earned.

So, they went back to the drawing board. After allowing the pianist to retire gracefully, they pooled the money of the combined salaries of her and the former choir director, and they hired the music minister of their dreams. He transformed the traditional chancel choir into a gospel choir, organized a multicultural community gospel sing on Sunday nights, hosted special concerts, invited guest artists, started an artist-in-residence program, and formed a few quartets and octets of young voices. Soon, the church pews began to fill up. So did the nursery and the children's Sunday school classes. Since I had been tasked with growing the church's membership, I looked like a genius. But this was one case where the biggest factor wasn't a system we put into place; it was an executive team moving the mission forward with some courage and ingenuity.

It may sound callous, but you can actually save money if you eliminate the position of several "amateurs" (basically paid volunteers) and hire a professional with expert skill, high efficiency, and the charisma to attract enough actual (unpaid) volunteers.

Music is probably the area where churches can make the quickest, easiest updates and improvements. You might be surprised by the number of award-winning artists who are open to helping a local church when they aren't on the road. The time between tours can get very lean, and many artists are happy to spend their time and pad their pockets by taking a temporary position.

I was once helping a church that had a temporary music minister with a chip on his shoulder. He wanted things to improve, but only if the improvements were based on his ideas.

We found an outstanding Christian recording artist who was willing to work there for six months. Everyone was excited to take the church's praise and worship to new levels.

Everyone but the temporary worship leader, that is. During a meeting, his argument was, "Not everyone will like that recording artist's kind of music"—basically a variation of "Somebody might get mad," the phrase I urged you to excise from your speech. Someone else immediately retorted, "Well, not everyone likes to hear *you* play!" That quieted the temporary worship leader.

As it turned out, no one was more thrilled than he when the recording artist came on board. Why? Because he had the benefit of learning from a professional. Plus, he was invited to play backup on the artist's next tour.

As Woody Hayes liked to say, "You win with people." Be sure to view your employees as assets instead of expenses. You get what you pay for; high-value assets produce higher-quality results. Top performers are accustomed to delivering results, and the outcomes you might only have dreamed of may be simple stuff to a professional. When interviewing potential candidates, don't assume that you can't afford those in the top tier. You might be surprised by the mountain peaks they will commit to achieve in exchange for the money they demand to be paid.

Minding His Business Basic Principle:

When interviewing potential candidates for a position, consider the possibilities and the potential before you estimate the cost.

CHAPTER 31

CHARACTER COUNTS

Who handles the interviewing and hiring in your church? Recruiting employees is a skill that improves with experience. One of the main differences between novice recruiters and seasoned recruiters may be seen in the way they report on the results of an interview. A novice recruiter will tell you what he thinks and how he feels; a seasoned recruiter will tell you what he learned and now knows.

As we have discussed several times in this book, a relational person put in charge of interviewing will focus on how a potential employee will fit in with the existing team. But it's also important to discern the candidate's knowledge, skills, passions, and—most important—character.

I have conducted thousands of interviews. While I usually allow the discussion to run its own course, there is a set of questions I always ask without fail, each one with a purpose to probe for important elements of character. After all, the "wrong" answer for one job might be the right answer for another.

One of these questions is a hypothetical scenario I present to the candidate. I say, "Imagine that you're a shift manager at a fast-food restaurant. One of your employees has fallen on hard economic times. Each month, he has to choose between buying medicine and food. One day, you catch him leaving work with an open case of hamburger. What do you do?"

There is no "right answer" to this scenario. If I am interviewing for the position of an accountant or a manager—someone charged with enforcing rules—the "right" answer might be, "I would turn him over to the police." If I am looking to hire a director of children's ministry or a youth leader, the "right" answer might be, "I would seek to counsel and correct the employee." You need to be uncompromisingly principled to be an accountant; you need an abundance of grace to be a youth leader. And the way the candidate responds will reveal his dominant character traits, which will assist you in determining whether he is the right person for the job.

Here is another question I always ask: "It is ten years from now, and you are wildly successful. What does that look like?" Again, there is no right answer. But the response of an ideal candidate should include some aspect of the job you are looking to hire him to do. If I am hiring an executive pastor, his ten-year vision should include leading some sort of ministry.

I also expect the candidate to respond in terms of "doing" rather than "having." A person who defines his success by how much money he has or the number and quality of his possessions will not be happy for very long doing the work of church and ministry.

In addition, I always assess whether the candidate is an extrovert or an introvert. Neither one is better than the other; it's simply smart to know what type you're hiring. If you are seeking a new chaplain for a hospital, for example, you want a good listener; and introverts tend to be better listeners than extroverts. If you are looking for someone to lead groups of people, you should probably hire an extrovert.

One way to determine whether someone is an extrovert or an introvert is to ask him what he does for fun. Extroverts tend to name favorite hobbies that include other people, high energy, and plenty of noise; introverts usually prefer activities that are quiet, calm, and performed in solitude.

Another way to find out whether someone is an extrovert or an introvert is to ask a simple question: "What happens when you get mad?" Extroverts get loud; introverts get quiet.

One key series of questions I always pose to potential employees has to do with honesty. First, I ask, "What is something you have done that you are very proud of?" The truth is, I don't care how he responds; this question is just a setup for the next question: "Tell me about a time when you failed at something."

The worst possible way to answer this question is, "I have never failed at anything." When I get this answer, the interview is over. I'll ask a few more questions just to be polite, but I don't need to hear another thing. A person who thinks he has never failed is not being honest with himself and will always redefine success in a way that makes him look good. He will not be open to constructive criticism and will never be happy unless he is the one in control. In short, he will be nothing but trouble.

The best answer to the question is, "Only one time I failed at something?" Again, the specific example he provides does not matter. What matters is how quickly he recalls a specific failure and how articulately he describes it, for this indicates that he has a realistic estimation of himself and enough maturity to admit responsibility when things go wrong on his watch.

The next question in this series is tougher: "What did you learn from this failure?" Again, the answer itself is not as important as the candidate's ability to respond swiftly and articulately, for this tells me that the interviewee dwelled on his failure until he gleaned a lesson from it. It tells me that he is a person with great potential for growth, and someone who isn't likely to make many repeat mistakes.

To conclude this line of questioning, I ask, "What was your contribution to the failure?" Most people find this question the most difficult to answer, but their ability to do so quickly and articulately indicates a person who is honest with himself. And that is a crucial quality, for someone who is not honest with himself will not be honest with me.

One of the primary ways I probe for experience is by asking people about things they have done that are pertinent to the job for which I am considering them. But instead of merely asking what they have done, I ask them to describe exactly how they did it. I often prompt candidates to describe for me how it would look if projected as a silent movie on a screen. If it's something they've done many times, they ought to be able to describe it in detail from memory without any problems.

I once worked with a church that was losing money every month. It was pretty clear to me that they were paying for a significant number of services that most churches assigned to volunteers.

I brought up the issue during a staff meeting. "Seems to me that you pay an awful lot of childcare workers on Sunday mornings," I said. "Why don't you use volunteers?"

"You need to get something straight," the children's minister piped up. "This is not thirty years ago. People are too busy to volunteer."

"We tried to start new life groups," the adult discipleship pastor put in, "but no one wants to volunteer to lead."

I said, "What if we hired a director of volunteer recruitment?" Everyone loved that idea. I hope you see the irony.

So, I set out to hire a volunteer recruitment coordinator for them. I asked one candidate what she considered to be the best way to recruit volunteers. Her answer was quick and to the point: "Call them or ask them face-to-face."

"Go on," I said.

"Anything else is a waste of time. E-mail, sign-up sheets, pew cards—none of these passive methods yields the results of good old face-to-face asking."

"Anything else?" I asked.

"Yeah. Whatever you do, don't hand out the big list of all the opportunities to volunteer unless you have a team ready to call people that week and put them in a position right away. Unless you're ready to act, it's a waste of money, and it tells the prospective volunteers that you don't really care."

My next question was this: "What are some non-negotiables to keep you interested in doing this job for us?"

"I don't want to seem rude, but I honestly don't want to work with a team that does not know how to treat its volunteers," she replied.

"And what does that look like?" I asked her.

"It looks like a bunch of church workers sitting around, saying, 'Nobody wants to volunteer,' when none of them has made a phone call to ask a new person to volunteer in a long time."

"Go on."

"People want to volunteer; they just want to be asked, not informed. I don't want to do a ton of work just to send a church leader a bunch of volunteers, only to have the leader turn them away because he has nothing for them to do. And he needs to take the time to show his appreciation for their helping out." She was getting animated.

"It sounds like that really bothers you."

"Don't get me started," she said.

Does this woman sound like a person you would want to hire to recruit volunteers? Would you be concerned that she might upset some other people on the staff? In this case, what I saw was a person who was experienced in recruiting volunteers in a church setting, knew how to get results, and was passionate. Sure, she was probably going to upset some church leaders. But I would just expect those people to adapt.

I hired her on the spot. What do you think happened to the church's volunteer recruitment efforts? Sign-ups went through the roof. And she was so successful that the rest of the staff struggled to keep up. After all, when you don't have volunteers to lead your church's life groups, you don't need to work hard on providing the life groups with new curriculum.

There is an old saying that goes, "What doesn't start right rarely ends right." Low productivity, poor morale, and high turn-over have more to do with poor hiring decisions than it does with poor leadership. Get the right person to conduct the interviews, and make sure he probes each candidate for character.

~

Minding His Business **Basic Principle:**

When recruiting, ask tough questions and be patient.
Hire character.

PART IV:

MARKETING AND FUND-RAISING

CHAPTER 32

"YOU" ARE NOT "THEM"

An old downtown church in a smaller city was one of the biggest in the area, with over two thousand members, as it entered the new millennium. Over the next ten years, however, attendance declined to between five and six hundred. The leadership came to realize that people were switching to local churches whose worship services were more contemporary.

The five-member church board called on me to help figure out what to do. They explained, "We can't stop the traditional worship service altogether. We can't shut down the choir. Many of the people coming still want the traditional worship style."

I suggested offering an alternative worship service. (I also suggested sending out a survey, but the board said they didn't want to upset people by asking questions—"someone might get mad," in other words.)

The remedy they came up with, hoping to have the best of both worlds, was to open a new campus on the other side of town. Most of the board members sang in the choir, and all the vocalists liked things the way they were, because they liked to sing. So, instead of asking around, the church board acted on a hunch informed by its own preferences rather than seeking to gather feedback from surveys and studies. With no input of any kind, they invested a great deal of money in launching a new worship center across town, with a new pastor and a "contemporary service," which was basically just another way of saying "without the choir."

The first Sunday of the contemporary service across town, the new worship center was packed. About three hundred church members had chosen to attend the service there, above and beyond a significant number of first-time visitors. Meanwhile, at the traditional service, attendance was around 270—and 70 of those people were in the choir.

The contemporary campus was an immediate success. It wasn't long before it separated completely from the original church, where attendance was dwindling. Today, the original church, with its traditional service, is just a remnant of what was once a great community of faith.

You can trace the demise of this great house of worship to the belief held by a *few* that their preferences were shared by the *majority*. The five members of the church board did not understand that they were not "everyone." To gauge the stance of the majority, you must collect empirical data—a process that requires time, resources, commitment, and skill. But until you look at the empirical evidence, the risk of making a shortsighted decision soars, as does the cost of failure.

I've heard well-meaning ministry leaders say, "Numbers don't matter; dollars don't matter; the mission matters." I have had my faith questioned many times for asking them questions such as, "How do you plan on paying for that?" or, "What if it does not work out the way you think it will?" Yes, the mission is the most important thing. Yes, we are a people of faith. But I have yet to find a vendor who will accept high ideals and unrelenting faith as payment instead of cash. If you don't believe me, go ahead and let an electric bill go unpaid; then see how much of the mission you can accomplish in the dark. Numbers matter. Income matters. Facts matter. And those are several key factors that contribute to the success of the mission.

Let me give you an example of an anecdotal opinion that isn't supported by empirical evidence. A prevailing opinion shared by most people is that everybody hates telemarketing calls. You probably don't like them. I know I rarely answer them. Nobody has ever prayed, "Please, God, let my child grow up to be a telemarketer." There are even laws to "protect" us from "evil" telemarketing firms. That must mean that our assumption is correct. Right?

Well, let's examine the empirical evidence. In the United States alone, telemarketing is a $20 billion industry that employs almost 500,000 people. Millions of telemarketing calls are made each day. If "everyone" hates telemarketing calls, then why do companies bother hiring telemarketers? Because people answer their phone and buy whatever it is that's being sold. Companies hire telemarketing firms because *telemarketing works.*

The only thing you *can* be sure of when someone says "no one," "never," "everyone," and other absolutes is that the person speaking is *convinced* of the truth of what he believes, even if it's invalid. The church needs leaders who know how to embrace people and their opinions without ignoring the truth. We need to seek empirical evidence.

A minister in his early twenties named Zach convinced a large church in his town to let him hold a Christian concert in their enormous worship center. I had a desire to help kids in that part of the city, so I decided to help Zach. I called a colleague of mine who owned a telemarketing firm and convinced him to donate five thousand robocalls. Elated, I called Zach.

I gave him what I thought was good news.

"Don, no one listens to robocalls," he replied. "Every time I get one, I hang up."

I said, "Zach, I'm trying to help you. These calls, and the list of young Christian concertgoers in the area, are free."

"Don, you are going to have to get it through your head that the days of growing a church with slick marketing and advertising are over," Zach told me. "Those old ways just don't work anymore."

"How many robocalls did you contract last year?" I asked him. "The reason I ask is because, if the voice on the phone is someone the call recipient recognizes, 50 to 70 percent of recipients will listen to the whole message. If no one listens to robocalls, then who are the 50 to 70 percent who are taking these calls?"

"Hey, I gotta go," Zach said. "I'll call you later."

Guess how well the concert went. He thought that since "everyone" he'd talked to was planning on attending, then it meant a lot of people would attend. He thought that "everyone" was just like him. After a pitiful turnout at the concert, he got discouraged and eventually left town. I never heard from him again.

Communication matters. I had great success helping a medium-sized church with a month-long canned food drive to benefit the poor. The team started off pretty adamant that their parishioners would balk if we tried calling and e-mailing them. So, I suggested they try their method for the first three weeks of the food drive and allow me to use mine for the final week.

For three weeks, they did what they always did: put an announcement in the weekly bulletin and had someone mention the food drive from behind the pulpit at every service. In preparation for the fourth week, I asked the pastor to give me half an hour of his time, during which I recorded a one-minute video and then a one-minute audio of him saying, "This is Pastor Joe. On this last Sunday of the food drive, it would be a big help if you could go to your pantry right now and put a few cans of food next to your front door so you don't forget to bring them to church on Sunday."

I sent an e-mail of the video, as well as a robocall of the audio recording, to the entire congregation the day before the final day of the drive. That Sunday, thirty cans of food were brought for every single can raised in the three previous weeks combined. And, church attendance was up that day, to boot! The difference was not just in the medium; the difference was in the understanding that the people in the pews, for the most part, are never anywhere near as informed or connected as the people on the platform and behind the pulpit, who are usually responsible for conveying the information multiple times and therefore become very familiar with it.

Now, when the average person in the pews heard the message about the food drive during a worship service, he probably approved of the idea of a food drive and even intended to bring some food. The disconnect happened for one or more of the following reasons: (1) Some people didn't hear the message at all. (2) Only a few people heard the message more than once. (3) Many people who intended to bring canned food simply forgot.

Thus, the last-minute robocall and e-mail with a message from the pastor reminding people to "act now" prompted a much more positive response. We delivered a message to "them" that was much different from the one we would have delivered if we were informing only ourselves. It's the most basic rule of direct marketing: *You are not them.*

We have to recognize the realities outside our own paradigms. Acting on our own opinions and feelings alone is novice behavior, at best; at worst, quite frankly, it's sheer laziness. Sometimes, common sense is the most uncommon thing around. No one person, uniquely and individually crafted by God, is "average." It takes a bunch of people added together to come up with an average.

~

Minding His Business Basic Principle:

You are not "them." Never assume "they" think what you think.

CHAPTER 33

UNDERSTAND CONVERSION COSTS

A town in the Midwest with an interstate freeway running through it had two large churches, one on either side of the high-way. And the two were at odds with each other on dozens of issues. The tension was clear to everyone who lived there, in the forms of competing billboards, television ads, and so forth.

The church on the west end of town had a board that was elected by the congregation. The pastor, a highly educated man, was more than adequate in the pulpit. The associate pastor was a seminary graduate with a keen sense of humor that kept Sunday services hopping. They had a large youth group led by another young seminary graduate. They boasted a weekly attendance total-ing about two thousand. Church finances were laid out in the open once each year for the entire membership to see. Rarely did they ask the members for money, except to request the annual "faith promise" that was mailed to the members' homes. The budget of about $3 million was created based on a percentage of the total faith promises received, in case some of the people who pledged happened to leave the church or move away. Each year, the church experienced growth primarily as a result of people either moving to the community or transferring from another church.

On the east side of town was a church that seemed to have sprung up overnight, born of a merger between two smaller churches. For their pastor, the congregation elected a local builder who had grown up in one of the area churches, where, years earlier, he had been asked to come on staff. When the two churches joined forces, they downsized their board and got rid of annual membership meetings. The first thing the pastor did was purchase a piece of property along the interstate and construct a large, contemporary-style building to house his congregation. He then took the two properties from the original churches and turned them into a primary and a secondary school. It wasn't long before they were incorporated as a school, with about one thousand local children enrolled.

Meanwhile, the pastor made appearances on local television and recorded radio messages that he always ended by inviting his viewers or listeners to receive Christ. On Sundays, in front of his home congregation, he drilled into them the charge to be a light in their community and, as such, to give money toward the church's evangelistic efforts. Over time, their budget grew to $10 million, church membership exceeded five thousand, and they reported bringing ten thousand souls to salvation per year.

Such claims rankled the leadership of the church on the west side of town. Their church was less bombastic, but they were doing great, with a beautiful campus, a solid congregation, and plenty of community outreach efforts, such as the youth group.

But were they justified in being rankled?

We can't reduce church work just to mere dollars and cents, of course; but let's return to an exercise we did in an earlier chapter and pretend that a church is an investment, and the return on that investment is the people it puts on a path to heaven. The large, established church on the west end did a solid work, provided services to new families in the area, and recorded about fifty salvations per year, all for a budget of $3 million. That comes to about $60,000 spent per soul saved. The church on the east side ballooned to a $10-million budget and had ten thousand salvations per year, mostly from their television and radio ministries. That comes to about a thousand dollars spent per soul saved. On average, about a thousand of those salvations happened in the church, meaning they spent about $10,000 per soul saved—still only a sixth of the cost of the older, more established church.

Both churches viewed each other as being "all about the money." The people who attended the west-side church were mostly affluent, reviewed their financials annually, and had a solid building that wasn't made of metal. They viewed those at the east-side church as greedy because the pastor was "always" asking for money to keep up with the enormous budget. And the people who attended the east-side church saw the west-side church as greedy because they spent almost every dollar they took in on themselves, in the form of programs and facilities.

How should we evaluate the "success" of the churches in question? It depends on the goals they set. The goal of God's kingdom on earth is to save people from their sins and make disciples of all nations. The bottom line is, how many lives are touched? How many people are reached? How much of the stated mission is accomplished, and with what degree of efficiency? By any of these standards, the east side church demonstrated greater success.

So, what is the cost of conversion, and where does the process begin? It begins with understanding the difference between an expense and an investment. An expense is something you pay for that yields nothing in return, at least directly. Examples of church expenses include office supplies and fuel for the pastors' vehicles. With an investment, on the other hand, there is an expectation of a return. In the example above, we measured the return in terms of the number of souls going to heaven each year. But let's put it in secular terms just to help us analyze it further.

Let's start with the amount that a member or a regular attender (someone who attends at least twenty-four times in a calendar year) gives to the church in a given year—say, $3,000. Then, let's go all the way back to when this individual became a member or a regular attender—the first time his or her name appeared on record with the church. We will call all such people "new names." Now, go back in your data records to three years ago and take a look at all the new names from that year. Some of them would have attended one time, given no money, and never returned. Others would have attended a few times, given a little, and then left. And still others would have become regular attenders and generous givers. Regardless, add up all the giving from this group of people over three years, and then divide that sum by the original number of new names that came on file three years ago. This will give you the average three-year value of a "new name," or a church visitor.

This is an extraordinarily important concept that will help you to allocate resources effectively in support of your mission. Let's say that your church saw three hundred new names three years ago. Over the next three years, that group gave money as outlined in the table below:

Group Contribution

Visits over three years	People	Over following three years	Three year value per new name
1	150	$150	$1
2-10	75	$3,500	$47
11-24	50	$12,000	$240
25+	25	$34,000	$1,360
	300	$49,650	$166

In our example above, 25 people went on to become regular tithing members, while 150 attended one time and were never seen again. Either way, collectively, they are worth about $166 per new name.

Now, let's say that you decide to host a concert at your church. The price of the band is $2,000, and publicity will cost an additional $2,000, for a total cost of $4,000. How many new names will you have to capture at the concert to have a three-year payoff on the event? The answer is 24 new names.

Here is the math:

$4,000 cost of concert / $166 three year value of a new name = 24

Without knowing the future value of a new name, the cost of the concert is an expense. Knowing the future value of a new name turns the $4,000 concert expense into an investment in church growth.

This calculation seems simplistic because it is that simple. I have done this math a thousand times. It always works out.

Many churches would probably say, "This is great, but we have no money. We can't afford to put on a concert." I would tell them they can't afford *not* to. Analyze your vacation Bible school this way. Analyze your potluck dinners and all the other events you put on. Find out if you're just spending money or if you're investing in something that will bring people to Jesus and grow your church.

One church I worked with ran an annual community flea market over Memorial Day weekend that cost them about $10,000. It was one of the largest annual events in that particular community, drawing thousands of people and also spiking attendance at the church for several weeks immediately following. After five years of running the flea market, the church experienced a time when money was tight, and they were talking about canceling the event. Their argument was that the small surge in attendance was not worth the expense.

I looked at their attendance records and did the math I just showed you. Each year since starting the flea market, they added about 700 new names over a twelve-month period. About 250 (36 percent) of those new names came on file in June—the month that immediately followed the scheduling of the flea market. Prior to starting the flea market, only about 50 new names came on file in the month of June each year.

Then I looked at the records of giving for the current year, specifically examining the current givers whose names had first appeared on file in the month of June over the past five years. What I saw was that this group represented about 15 percent of the church's current givers. In five years, the church spent a total of $50,000 on the Memorial Day flea market. In the present year alone, they had received close to $75,000 from people whose names had first appeared on file shortly after one of the past five Memorial Day flea markets. When I presented this information to the church board, they decided not to cancel the flea market.

I hope that this example colors the way you view your church's budget and growth. Investing in the acquisition of "new names" yields big returns, both in the now, financially, and for eternity.

⌒

Minding His Business Basic Principle:

Understand your conversion cost before you make financial decisions (and definitely before you throw stones at the other church across town).

CHAPTER 34

"I NEVER..."

In making decisions, one cannot afford to confuse anecdotal information with empirical evidence. Jesus said that we would "know them by their fruit" (see Matthew 7:16–20), which means, "Look at the fruit"—i.e., "Look at what is observable." In science, it is called "empirical evidence." Anecdotal information is unproven and generally colored by the opinion of the person giving it.

It's common for any given group to use shorthand to make their point. They'll say, "everybody knows such-and-such," "nobody does such-and-such," "people never do such-and-such." These are the marks of anecdotal information.

I sat in several meetings with a young staff member who was continually making comments based on anecdotal information. At one of these meetings, he said, "We should stop e-mailing our congregation. E-mailing is old-school. Who reads e-mails anymore?"

E-mail was an important aspect of our strategy to convert "new names" (first-time visitors) into members. I couldn't allow his remark to go unchallenged.

"Can you answer something for me?" I said.

"Sure." He leaned forward, clearly ready to proffer more of his insights.

"We have gone from three hundred e-mail addresses on file to three thousand in the past year. If no one wants to be e-mailed, why have so many people given us their e-mail address?"

"Well," he said, backpedaling, "we e-mail way too much."

"Can you answer something else for me?" I said. "We send a congregation-wide e-mail once a week, on average; and our rate of people asking to unsubscribe is almost zero. Why is that, do you suppose?"

He talked for the next five minutes. I'm not sure what he said; I am sure he did not answer my question.

The truth was, he didn't read *his* e-mails. That is not surprising. Most empirical research shows that the younger you are, the less likely you are to use e-mail as a primary mode of communication. But that doesn't mean that "nobody" ever reads his e-mail.

When it comes to church communications, people's preferences vary. Some prefer e-mail; others prefer getting their updates via the church bulletin; and still others use social media on their smartphone. That's why every smart church has a "multimedia" communication strategy—so that each member has access to whatever message the church leadership wants to convey via his preferred channel, whether e-mail, texting, "snail mail," bulletin announcements, phone calls, and so forth.

Too many church leaders make changes based on anecdotal information. The anecdotal kills the spaghetti dinner. Let me show you what I mean.

Let's say that a church decides to host a spaghetti dinner. The event coordinators place an announcement in the bulletin for a few weeks, and the pastor publicizes the event during the announcements portion of the Sunday service one week prior to the event.

The assumption is that "everybody knows." And so, when next to no one shows up for the spaghetti dinner, the organizers reach the anecdotal conclusion that no one likes spaghetti dinners. As a result, they decide not to plan another one next year.

What they failed to consider is that they might have done an inadequate job of publicizing the event. Let me give you a couple of points based on empirical evidence. First, about 20 percent of the people in attendance at a given worship service come to church less than one time per month. This fact alone should incline us to announce an event at four consecutive services if we want to be sure that "everyone" has a chance of hearing about the event at least once.

Second, even if everyone hears the message once, to assume that their absence from the spaghetti dinner indicates a dislike of such events is foolish and fallacious. Some people are merely forgetful and need to hear a message more than once to remember it.

My anecdotal opinion is that the first person to conclude that no one likes spaghetti dinners probably had a significant role in organizing and promoting the event—and did it poorly.

We also have to consider the skill of the people crafting the communication. The most common mistake churches make in their communication strategies is assuming that everyone is listening and has understood. We need to craft all communication as if the person on the receiving end knows nothing about the subject and has no comprehension of what we are describing. The communication strategy of most churches is to deliver invitations, not advertisements. An invitation assumes people want to come, that they know what they are being invited to, and that all they need to know is where and when. But an advertisement also answers what and why—in essence, what's in it for them.

There are many gifted speakers but few gifted listeners. It doesn't matter what you think you said; it's only what is heard

that has been communicated. That's why it is extremely important to recognize that announcing something once from the pulpit
is no guarantee of anyone hearing, let alone understanding and
retaining.

Far too many decisions are made based on opinion rather than
empirical evidence. Today, most of us have access to hundreds of
thousands of opinions with the click of a link on the Internet. The
interconnectedness of the world, and the easy access to information (as well as to the means of sharing information), gives the illusion that every opinion is worthy of being published and read by
millions; thus, many people tend to base their decisions on popular opinion rather than fact. But not all opinions are created equal.
When meeting with people who speak in terms of "I think" or "I
feel," it's important to get to the bottom of the actual data before
making a decision.

Recently, I was sitting in a meeting with some ministry leaders
discussing some marketing, membership, and fund-raising strategies that all hinged on getting a letter sent out in time. It was
November, and I cautioned them, "When we get to these dates
around the holidays, send your third-class mail a week earlier
than you normally would, because the mail slows down during the
holidays."

"That doesn't make any difference," one young leader said.

"It doesn't?" I was incredulous. I'd been sending direct mail
since long before he was born. In my career, I have mailed out over
a billion pieces through snail mail. That's actually a conservative
estimate, considering that I've managed printing companies and
letter shops, besides being involved in marketing and nonprofit
fund-raising for decades.

Either way, the empirical fact is that there are a finite number
of cubic inches in a mailbox, a finite number of cubic feet in
a mail truck, and a finite number of pounds that a mail carrier

can transport. On top of all this, add Christmas cards, catalogs, holiday sale advertisements, year-end requests from charities, and packages to friends and loved ones...the U.S. Postal Service absolutely slows down its deliveries of third-class mail during the holidays.

"No, the mail never goes late at Christmastime," the young leader insisted.

"That hasn't been my experience," I said.

"Well, that's your opinion," he said. "But it never takes longer at Christmas."

Wow. I was speechless.

It came as no surprise to me when the pastor's year-end letter asking for Christmas presents for orphans arrived in the congregants' mailboxes during the first week of January. Needless to say, they did not get very many donations for Christmas presents.

⌒

Minding His Business **Basic Principle:**

When you hear such absolute terms as "never," "always," "no one," and "everyone," ask to see the data before making a decision.

CHAPTER 35

ASK NOT AND RECEIVE NOT

My favorite part of an airplane flight is the landing. I don't like getting on planes. I am very fond of getting off them. But I've found that if your number of takeoffs matches your number of landings, in most cases, you're going to be okay.

But on one particular day, I would have rather stayed in the air than land in the city where I had been summoned for a meeting. An old friend of mine pastored a large church that had spent the past eight years on a slow, steady march toward extinction. For the past ten-plus years, the church leadership had put little effort and creativity into asking the congregants for money. From time to time, the pastor would merely say something along the lines of, "If you feel inspired to give, please fill out a form."

When he finally acknowledged that he needed to raise some serious money, he called me in to help. At my first meeting with the leadership team—including the director of facilities, the book-keeper, the children's minister, and the youth pastor—the pastor went around the room and asked each person what he or she thought of asking the members for money.

"Let's not press people too hard, or they're likely to leave," a couple of them said.

I was ready for this response, and I asked them, "How many people will leave if you ask for money? Do you know how many of your people won't give as much as a dime unless they're asked? Can we look at the records to see if there are more of those than there are people who are likely to leave?"

"We can look at the records, but we know our people," one staffer said. "They'll leave."

"Some people will never give anything, whether we ask or not," I said, "but they'll still leave the church. Know why? Because, if you stay on the financial path you're on, this church will one day have to close its doors, and then anyone who's left will be forced to leave. So, if they're going to leave eventually, anyway, why not ask them for money now and risk having them leave before you're obligated to close the doors for good?"

Privately, the pastor and I looked through the staff members' giving records. Of the two staff people who were the most adamant against asking the congregation for money, one did not give at all, and the other gave less than 2 percent of his income. And they decided to try to sway the decision in their favor so that they would never be asked to give.

That pastor is still a good friend of mine, but he couldn't turn that church around. He finally resigned, and the church ended up closing its doors.

I realize that the majority of churches have a hard time requesting money from their members. One reason I hear fairly often is this: "I don't ask for money because people don't like being asked for money." In most cases, what these people really mean is, "I don't ask for money because *I* don't like asking for money." Well, who does? The truth is, asking for money is part of our mission in spreading the gospel. We aren't preaching the full gospel if we aren't preaching about money.

Remember that, during His earthly ministry, Jesus talked more about money than He did about heaven or hell. We aren't afraid to ask people to love their neighbor, to serve others, or to read their Bibles; we just don't want to ask them to give money. Money is important to God for only one reason—because it's one of our most precious tangible possessions. Back in Old Testament times, people had to sacrifice a fatted calf or a lamb or a dove as "payment" for their sins. Today, we don't need to purchase salvation or forgiveness; but God does want us to have enough faith to give freely of our precious possessions, our money, to those in need and toward the advancement of His kingdom on earth.

God asks us for a modest 10 percent of our income. If He asked for 1 percent, we wouldn't notice it much. Giving 50 percent would be a heavy load. Ten percent is enough to make us swallow hard, but not enough to break the bank. We don't lose our "stuff"—our car, our house, our pantry. Giving 10 percent is a huge step of faith when you start, but then it grows your faith.

As part of your church leadership team, you need to trust God enough to risk failure. Only 2 percent of Americans actually tithe based on their gross income (before taxes). So, what do you do? Trust God enough to risk failure. Either God is who He says He is, or He isn't. Either God's Word is true, or it is not.

Being faithful to this part of God's Word makes the church blessed. Raising money fearlessly is part of spreading the gospel. The apostle Paul said in Romans 1:16, *"I am not ashamed of the gospel, because it is the power of God that brings salvation to everyone who believes."* So, why would you, or any Christian leader, be ashamed to ask people for a tithe?

God handed down 613 laws in the Old Testament, some of them as detailed as specifying how one ought to wash his body. And keeping those laws was so difficult, people had to really want to obey. It took a great deal of faith to keep all those laws. In the New Testament, God set us free from those requirements. But the desire to obey is still paramount. Giving our tithes and offerings today, we have to really want to obey God. God doesn't want our money; He just wants our willingness to trust Him enough to part with it.

A church in the Midwest had yellow-tinted windows installed in the 1960s as a temporary measure until they could collect enough money for stained glass—which they never did. The aging building and overgrown yard saw little care, all because the back door is where all the "business" occurred—where local people in need showed up for free clothes and staples from the food pantry.

I was called in to help the church develop a communication strategy to attract a younger crowd and boost attendance, but I quickly determined that their priority needed to be revamping the building and grounds—something they couldn't do without raising extra money, since almost all their available funds went toward feeding the hungry and clothing the naked.

I encouraged the pastor to ask his congregation for money to put toward the updates the church so desperately needed. What better way for that congregation to spend money than on a venture that would help them grow and, in turn, give them the ability to help even more people by both meeting their physical needs and leading them to spiritual salvation? When a church or a ministry is doing obvious good, it should be hard *not* to ask for money.

⁓

Minding His Business Basic Principle:

Giving grows faith. Help your congregants grow their faith by challenging them to give.

CHAPTER 36

BELIEVE MALACHI 3:10

I have yet to hear someone say, "Boy, do I regret tithing." For many people, tithing is the biggest step of faith they will ever take; but the faith that it builds will permeate every aspect of their lives and also bless generations of people to come. Why are we so hesitant to ask people to do something that will benefit them so richly, in addition to enriching the church?

I traveled to the West Coast to help a mainline Protestant church that drew about four hundred people to its Sunday services. They had an annual "pledge Sunday"; the rest of the year, they kept the pews stocked with offering envelopes and would, on occasion, remind the people to use them as they felt led.

The church leadership team had big plans that would require major funding. Therein lay their biggest problem. There were many young families in the congregation, but only a few members tithed faithfully. This is the first issue the leadership agreed to address.

The pastor was a good expositor, so I asked him to unpack just one verse over the next four Sundays. The verse was Malachi 3:10:

"Bring the whole tithe into the storehouse, that there may be food in my house. Test me in this," says the LORD ALMIGHTY, "and see if I will not throw open the floodgates of heaven and pour out so much blessing that there will not be room enough to store it."

The pastor explained to his congregants, "All through Scripture, God tells us not to test Him. But one time in Scripture, God says, 'Test me in this.'" He went on to say that in Malachi 3:10, the phrase *"test me in this"* is both a command and a promise. In the rest of the Old Testament, God tells His people to "do this... because I am God." Only in Malachi does He say, "Test me...and I will...." Money and possessions are universal. Almost everyone has something, of which he can part with a tenth. This means that the promise of Malachi 3:10 is available to everyone. The pastor had enough faith that God was who He said He was, and that His Word was true, to preach the principle of Malachi 3:10.

At the end of each message on Malachi 3:10, the pastor asked the people to give money to alleviate a famine that was devastating a people group in Africa. He would say, "For the price of a cup of coffee, you can feed a family in Africa for a day. If you don't want to give a tithe or make a pledge, how about giving up a cup of coffee a day? Just fast one purchased beverage a day and put the money in a jar; then, once a week, bring your money to church to add to the bucket."

During a church board meeting, one member pointed out, "We're asking people to start giving, but we, as an organization, aren't giving."

A great deal of conversation ensued; and when the pastor took the pulpit the following Sunday, he made this announcement: "We've saved thousands of dollars for our building. But the elders believe we should match our faith with yours and send everything to Africa, along with the results of your sacrificial giving."

The giving had increased week by week, but it exploded that Sunday. Including the building fund proceeds, they raised a total of $45,000—enough to fill a 40,000-pound container of food and send it to the people suffering from the famine. Throughout this campaign, giving went up about 25 percent.

Then the pastor said, "If you're not tithing, take a step of faith and give more. Take your income and see what a tenth would look like. Then, do just part of that—perhaps a tenth of a tenth, a mere 1 percent of your income. If everyone gave even just 1 percent more of his income, it would double our annual budget."

The pastor went on, "If you are wondering about how much God wants you to give, keep thinking of a bigger number until the number in your mind makes you swallow hard. If the gift does not make you swallow hard, it does not take faith to give it."

The people got excited about giving. The leadership followed the giving drive with a membership campaign. Within a year, they were seeing real growth in terms of attendance, as well as revenue. There was plenty of money to fund the needs of the facility and also to cover the outreach events they planned. They were blessed because they tested God on Malachi 3:10.

Another time, a pastor whose church's account was down to its last $10,000 threw up his hands. "Don, you figure out how to raise the money!" he said.

I challenged him to preach Malachi 3:10. "If you believe the Bible is the inspired Word," I said, "and God says, 'Test me in this,' then why should we be ashamed to ask and test Him?"

The pastor just looked at me.

"Read the verse!" I said. "He doesn't even say 'please'! He just says, 'Test me'!"

The next time this pastor took the pulpit, I was in attendance. He brought an outstanding message based on Malachi 3:10. We went on to craft a solid campaign around the message series. But then he surprised me. He said, "If I'm going to preach it, then we're going to live it. Give the rest of our money away."

Twenty years earlier, I would have thought, *Have you lost your mind?* But now, I wondered, *How could God not honor that?* God had to be faithful to to this act of faith.

I was with the pastor when he wrote a check for $12,000 to assist the victims of Hurricane Katrina. He paid his staff, then gave the rest away. He emptied the bank account. The campaign continued, and money kept coming in; within one quarter, the church finances were back to where they'd been at the start. Within a year, the church was completely solvent. Within two years, most of the debts the church had incurred during the "lean years" had been paid off.

Again, God does not need our money. He just wants us to develop a faith that's big enough to trust Him as we give it away. For God to pass the test He set up for Himself, He has to respond to our tithing by pouring out abundance on our households.

Every pastor must have enough faith to teach this principle and trust God to do what He said He would do. Yet countless pastors neglect to ask because they fear making their congregants uncomfortable. They need to remember that we serve a God who says the stars and planets are but vapor in His breath. Your finances may be a big deal to you, but never to God. Trust Him. Test Him.

~

Minding His Business Basic Principle:

You might doubt that your congregation has enough faith to give, but the problem might be that you don't have enough faith to ask them to give.

CHAPTER 37

GIVING IS A DECISION THE CHURCH SHOULD MAKE EASY

John Wesley's method of ministry was to go to where the people were. He wanted to make his ministry as accessible as possible. And this ought to be the church's attitude toward giving, too. In any given congregation, there will be different demographics; your job is to make it easy for them to give in the way that is most relevant to them.

The most important thing to remember is that people give for a variety of reasons, most of which have more to do with where they are on their faith journey than with their financial capacity to give. Giving is never a matter of "one size fits all." And understanding the different reasons that motivate people's giving will help the church craft the most effective methods and mechanisms in their appeals for money.

Most mature givers give because their faith requires it. They have taken God at His word, tested Him, and found Him faithful. This group of people will give regardless of what the church does or how it asks. At the other end of the spectrum are people who show up to church a few times a year and drop only a couple of dollars in the offering plate.

Giving, like faith, is a journey that spans a lifetime. Faith grows with time, and giving grows in proportion to one's faith. It is an observable, tangible evidence of spiritual maturity (or the lack thereof). But, just as important, giving also prompts the growth of faith. Recognizing this truth can help you, as a church leader, to craft strategies of both requesting and receiving money that are also designed to increase the giver's spiritual maturity.

For example, studies show that millennials—those between twenty-five and forty years of age—prefer high-tech methods of giving money. If you don't offer them the options of making autopayments or giving via text messaging, they'll look at you as if your head is on backward. Most of them don't know where their checkbooks are. They certainly don't carry them around in their pockets. Furthermore, this group of people is attracted to noble causes. Imagine standing in worship and talking about a humanitarian relief project you want to fund. Now, tell everyone to hold up his smartphone and text "$15" to the specific number associated with that project. Many more people, especially the millennials, are likely to give spontaneously. With this kind of giving, don't concern yourself with the amount. Rather, view spontaneous giving as a chance to help people grow in their faith, as well as to expand the church's donor base. The technology that supports text-to-give is readily available and affordable; all it takes is someone in your ministry who's willing to handle the legwork.

Most of the time, a decision to give is, at its core, emotional and spontaneous. That being said, when someone makes a decision to give, you want to be ready to transact the donation as quickly and as simply as possible. For example, if you send out a letter requesting donations, be sure to include a self-addressed, postage-paid envelope. The last thing you want is to require people to go look for a pen, an envelope, and a stamp when they decide to spontaneously give. Also, you should keep the message short and the font large. If you have to expand the margins and reduce the font size to get all the words to fit on the page, you've said far too much. Moreover, the most common respondents to direct mail tend to be elderly. Using a large font size means they won't have to go looking for their glasses in order to read your letter.

To reach those who are more technologically inclined, be sure that every e-mail request for money includes a "donate now" button for electronic giving, linked to a secure Web page that accepts at least several different types of credit card. You should also give site users the option of having their card information saved for future donations.

One word of caution here: Don't save any credit card or banking information on your system(s). Hire a transaction merchant that is PCI-compliant. All the reputable companies offer templates that you can customize with your church logo.

Two other important options to offer on every solicitation mechanism you use are: (1) "Would you like to make this a monthly donation?" and (2) "Would you like to create an auto check or auto deduction for your giving?" In the average church, when people miss a Sunday service, only about 2 percent will make up for having missed the offering plate. But 100 percent of the contributions from auto-givers are received, regardless of their presence at church on Sunday. This onetime decision has a positive impact on people's giving for years to come. Including these two statements with every request for money will yield significant returns in the long run.

A large suburban church in the Southwest that routinely asked its members for money wanted my company to review its strategies and offer insights on how to improve them. We added the "auto-give" option to their Web site, then worked with their communications team members to integrate the option into every type of church literature and communication mode. In addition, we trained their staff to mention the option in their telephone conversations. The strategy was simply to ask, "Would you like to do your giving by auto check or auto deduct?" It wasn't a hard push. There was one box to check on a form, one button to click on a Web site, or one simple question to answer.

With constant reminders of these options, over the course of two years, 20 percent of the congregants were giving via auto deduct or auto check. And from those who were already regular givers before they started using auto-deduct, donations spiked over 25 percent. And all this just from asking a couple simple questions.

Another opportunity to enhance giving comes when you receive new members. Most churches require new members to attend a series of membership classes. Whatever type of introduction your church provides, be sure to make it clear that yours is a church that lives by Malachi 3:10. Teach the principle of giving and explain why the new members should expect to be asked to grow their faith by giving. Illustrate for them how their giving will go to support the entire ministry. Show them all the good that your church does. Then, present to them all the options they have when it comes to giving: check, credit card, smartphone app, text-to-give, and so forth.

An important concept to keep in mind is that giving involves at least three decisions:

1. Whether to give
2. How often to give
3. How much to give

In regard to the third decision, you will always bring in more money if you allow donors to select a specific amount rather than asking them to "fill in the blank." For example, first, ask for a tithe (10 percent). If the donor does not think he is ready to give that amount, ask him to consider giving 1 percent more than he currently gives. If that does not work, ask him to pledge any amount to be given regularly over time. If that does not work, ask him to fast one purchased beverage a day and give the money to a ministry that feeds hungry people, instead. The latter will not help the general budget, but it will take an attendee and turn him into a giver, thereby beginning his journey toward generous giving. Next, ask him to identify his position on a list of giving thresholds, and ask him to consider moving up one step. Ask him to write down an amount and to submit it. Then, have a pastor call or visit him the following week to pray with him over the commitment that God will bless him and grow his faith through his generous step of faith.

A church was organizing a major event for their men's ministry, and they calculated that they would need to charge each attendee $40 in order to break even. So, they posted the $40 admission on the Web site and on every piece of promotional material they created for the event. Also on the Web site, they featured a button that would allow visitors, by a single click, to contribute toward a scholarship fund that would grant admission to men who couldn't afford to attend. In the end, they collected $48 for every man who attended.

The men's event was a huge success. Lives were changed, and families were blessed. During the event, the pastor challenged the attendees, asking them to think of a man they knew who could benefit from the same experience. Then, he told them that, in exchange for the name and contact information of that person, they would receive a DVD recording of the event, plus free admission to the next men's event. The following year, the event was in the black before they even opened the doors. All because they asked for $40, specifically, instead of letting the donor decide.

Christians need to learn to become givers, and the church needs to help them. Teach them the principle of testing God. Offer them multiple ways to make a positive difference in the world by their financial support. Give them various options of avenues through which to give. Ask them to give. Then, ask them to give again.

⌒

Minding His Business Basic Principle:

Ask people to give, then make it easy for them to do so.

CHAPTER 38

UNICORNS AND FAIRY DUST

I have heard the same discussion in so many ministry settings that, regardless of the particulars of a given example, they've all merged together in my mind as one goofy metaphor. It goes something like this:

"How are we going to make this thing a success?"

"I know exactly what we need! We need a horse."

"Why get a horse? Zebras are much prettier."

"Have you ever seen a unicorn? People love unicorns."

"Let's get two unicorns and some fairy dust!"

"But glitter is cheaper than fairy dust."

"Nah, we gotta have fairy dust to make it authentic."

"You can buy six horses for the price of a one-hour rental of a unicorn and a teaspoon of fairy dust."

"Look. Horses and glitter may have worked a long time ago, but anyone who knows anything about church growth knows that nothing grows without unicorns and fairy dust."

"But—"

"I can't believe you don't love Jesus."

In a few short moments, a brainstorm of ways to promote a church bake sale becomes an argument that the guy who dared to suggest that fair trade coffee isn't worth $18-a-pound is probably not bound for heaven; then, the leaders who deem $18-a-pound coffee outrageous decide to buy generic-brand beans, with the result that everyone believes them to be money-grubbers who don't care about the plight of the South American agricultural worker.

In many churches, a committee deems certain expenditures necessary to reach, teach, feed, or otherwise fulfill the mission when, in fact, these purchases probably won't make much of an impact, if any, on outcomes. I highly doubt that the type of coffee served at a church luncheon ever determined the destination of anyone's soul. How much time and money has the church wasted by debating the ethics of fairy dust over glitter? And, if we are keeping it real, the personnel asking for the "fairy dust" would probably never use their own money to purchase fairy dust at a cost of six horses per teaspoon.

Businesspeople don't think twice about acquiring and selling fairy dust, as long as the incremental return exceeds the incremental cost. They don't worry about selling teenagers tennis shoes that cost more than those teens' parents earn in a week. They don't worry about paying a ballplayer millions of dollars while hiking prices on ticket sales to the general public in order to make a profit. That's a different world—a world of unicorns and fairy dust. The church cannot afford to be sucked into the excesses of the secular world.

A church on the East Coast was working on a membership campaign. The congregation was located in a growing suburb that had once served as a bedroom community to a large city. Then, some large businesses moved in, and the community sprouted wings of its own. Soon, people were flocking to the suburb for jobs. New people were walking through the door of the church every week.

The church was stable, with plenty of room to grow. The pastor was a great communicator. All they had to do was convert visitors into members.

When they called me in to help, I laid out a plan, then sat in on some meetings with the committees that would be executing the plan.

The hospitality committee was filled with eager, bright, young career-minded people. Their first great idea was to have roving greeters strategically placed to help visitors find the children's area, the restrooms, the sanctuary, the information desk, and every other place that a first-timer might need. Then, the inevitable happened: Everyone on the committee piped up with his own idea of how to run a hospitality ministry.

"*How will the greeters be recognizable as such to the visitors?*"

"*They could wear bright vests, like the parking lot attendants.*"

"*Then they'll look like parking lot attendants. How about giving them T-shirts?*"

"*People don't like wearing T-shirts on Sundays. What about polo shirts, instead?*"

"*We have company shirts where I work. They're oxford shirts embroidered with the business logo. We all like them well enough to wear even when we're not at work.*"

"*Those would look sharp, and they'd go well with slacks for men and skirts for women.*"

"*We could have the hospitality logo embroidered on them. That would really look nice.*"

Finally, my observational skills were exhausted, and I had to become a participant.

"Look," I told them. "We just went from a hundred-and-fifty-dollar investment in vests to thousands of dollars' worth of oxford shirts. These often go home with volunteers and don't come back. Plus, you have to purchase so many different sizes. What are you going to do when John Jones, who is six foot five, turns in his shirt, but you have Jane Smith, who is five foot three, replacing him?"

The committee members started arguing the merits of their ideas that were a sum total of fifteen minutes old. Two of them got frustrated with anyone who dared to agree with what I'd said. One person became so frustrated, she walked out of the meeting.

"We need to keep our eye on the ball here," I reminded the remaining members. "What's most important is that the people walking through your doors for the first time feel welcome and make some sort of connection. What do you think will accomplish this better: a motivated, well-trained team of volunteers, or forty-dollar oxford shirts with embroidered logos?"

"You don't understand, Don," someone said. "This is the twenty-first century. Everybody knows image matters." (When you hear "everybody knows," remember, "you" are not "them.")

I replied, "Well, in that case, I am sure you will have no problem finding a large group of people who agree with you and are willing to donate the money to buy the first round of shirts, plus another group to pledge for the ongoing supply of shirts and custom embroidery. If 'everyone' agrees, we should have no problem getting a portion of 'everyone' to donate. How much can I put everyone here down for?"

Nobody spoke up. So, I suggested that we take the thousand dollars' worth of oxford shirts we'd just saved and use it to beef up our outreach into the community, so that there would plenty of visitors for the hospitality team members to greet. That got them happy again.

The voice of reason may have won out that day, even if I'm not sure I made any new fans. I think some of the hospitality committee members are still complaining about "that consultant who thought only about money."

I recently heard a sobering church statistic: 42 percent of U.S. churches go as much as one year without a single new profession of faith. While the church is fussing over unicorns and fairy dust, the people are perishing. I'm not sure which does more damage: spending resources on untested, unproven, unmeasured unicorns and fairy dust, or endlessly arguing the merits of the same. Too often, the local church is wrapped up in unicorns and fairy dust, while the local community lives in darkness.

Minding His Business **Basic Principle:**

Get your priorities in the proper order. When the lost are saved, the hungry are fed, the naked are clothed, and the captives are set free, then that is the time to talk about unicorns and fairy dust.

CHAPTER 39

YOUR GREATEST ASSETS

Two of a nonprofit's most valuable assets, from a business perspective, cannot be found on the balance sheet. The first one is the nonprofit status itself—the governmental 501(c)(3) status, which exempts revenue from taxation for the organization and its donors alike. As a church, you don't absolutely need the 501(c)(3), so your most profitable asset is this second one. Probably the most overlooked asset is the database of donors and attendees. Failing to secure that first asset can lead to a nonprofit's being shut down. And failing to safeguard the second asset can prove just as fatal.

Churches should invest in managing and maintaining their database, as it stores empirical evidence of the behaviors, desires, and contact information of people with a great or a growing affinity to your organization. And when you combine your attendance data with your data on donations and solicitation, your database becomes a fund-raising asset unlike any other.

Your database will actually direct you toward making money if you know the right questions to ask and how to find the answers.

In your database lie the answers to questions such as these:

1. Who supports us?

2. What do our supporters like? Dislike?

3. Who is satisfied or dissatisfied with us?

4. Who is growing with us?

5. Who is leaving us?

6. Who is ready to give (more)?

7. How should we ask them to do so?

8. Who should ask them, and when?

None of these answers should be new knowledge. Yet it is knowledge that many churches do not possess; or, worse, think they possess it and don't. Many churches will not even entertain concepts like direct marketing, database solicitation, predictive analytics, or data mining, because these methods seem "manipulative" or "too businesslike." I wonder how many of the people who don't like the idea of monetizing a database would feel the same way if it were their money, or if they could see how a lack of money means fewer people hearing the gospel, fewer hungry people getting fed, fewer naked people being clothed, and fewer captives being set free.

Let me ask you a question that you ought to be able to answer if your church practices proper data management. What percentage of your donors are giving 20 percent less money this year than they did last year? And is it just because their average gift amount is less, or there are fewer gifts coming in? Smaller average gifts tend to indicate that a donor has less money to donate, while fewer gifts, combined with declining attendance, indicates a declining affinity for your ministry. Or, there might be families in your church that are suffering severe problems that you'll never know about unless you look at the giving data. Did a family stop giving completely following a recent storm? Place a call and be the church.

A fairly large church with a decent-sized e-mail list asked for my help in growing its attendance. After making some of my routine checks, I asked to see the login table for the e-mail service itself. Then I asked how many people had the credentials to access the database and send electronic communication to the people on it. The person who handled the list looked into the account and found almost forty people who had full access to the list of contact information. One of the ministers who heard we were investigating database access became very belligerent about the consultant's "snooping." She was afraid that her credentials were about to be revoked.

We pressed on and kept probing. Multiple people with access rights had given their login information to church volunteers, so we really didn't know how many people actually had access to the contact information that thousands of people had entrusted to the church. I ran the names of those we knew past the accounting department and learned that twenty-two of them were former staff members who might have turned in their keys to the church but had never been taken off the list that gave them the keys to the contact database.

Then, we started auditing e-mails and other donor communications. One thing we saw right off the bat was a weekly export of new names to two different e-mail addresses. What we found was that one of the people receiving the weekly update was a church member who sold insurance. So, we loaded a bogus new name into the system; sure enough, the next week, we received a phone call and some literature in the mail from the insurance salesman. The second export was to the staff member who had expressed concern over my review of the login credentials for the database. As it turned out, she ran a multilevel marketing business that sold nutritional products on the side. She'd been heisting the e-mail addresses of new visitors and trying to make sales and to recruit new MLM "distributors." Worse, she'd been telling each new prospect that the pastor had asked her to call and that the church would benefit from the sale of her product. Neither was true.

When we confronted her, she said, "Don't you trust me?" The pastor didn't fire her because the situation was not exactly cut-and-dried; the church did not have a non-disclosure/non-compete agreement with its employees, and so many people had access to the database, it was hard to claim there was a proprietary nature to the system. However, she didn't stay long at the church after we terminated her access to the e-mail list. Apparently, her job there wasn't lucrative enough without the sales leads it had been providing.

On a side note, every church should include a confidentiality clause in its employment agreements and in all volunteer sign-up sheets in order to protect its data. And every church needs to protect access to its database as strictly as if it were guarding the U.S. Mint. If you are asking yourself, *What's the worst that could happen if someone unauthorized got access to our contacts list?* then read on.

There was a large denominational church in a smaller city that operated a school for pre-K through twelfth grade that was a huge drain on the church's budget. Like most Christian schools that include high school, they were constantly trying to find ways to raise money or cut costs. Private high schools are much more expensive to run than K-8 institutions.

We started down the path of putting their Web site and digital database to work for fund-raising for them.

"Hey," the school principal said in a staff meeting. "We have a kid who is a junior in high school who comes from a disadvantaged background, but he's smart with computers. What if we gave him free tuition in exchange for working as our Web and e-mail technologist and for helping the church, as well?"

Wow, what a bad idea. But once it was on the table, the principal fixated on finding a way to keep a kid in school while helping grow the church's budget. Others sided with him, and soon they had a seventeen-year-old Web and e-mail administrator.

The first thing that went wrong was that everyone on staff who experienced a computer problem needed help during office hours—which, of course, coincided with the student's class schedule. They needed an immediate fix in order to get their work done, but the school would not permit the student to leave class to offer assistance. Productivity plummeted.

The second thing to go wrong was that the church staff failed to realize that a teenager who's technologically intelligent doesn't usually respond well to taking orders.

The third problem was that the administrative security needed to be tightened up. I tried to convince them that too many people had access, but the young man wouldn't listen. "Just because you don't trust anyone doesn't mean people are dishonest," he said.

Regardless of what we said, he wouldn't tighten up, which led to the fourth problem: He hired his friends as subordinates, and those friends gave their pass codes to volunteers, many of whom were also their friends. All of a sudden, the church had a couple dozen teenagers with login credentials to its Web site, Facebook account, donor database, and giving records. Do you see where this is headed?

One of the teenage volunteers went on the Internet at the church and downloaded pornography. The pornography site embedded a peer-to-peer virus that turned the church server into a distribution node for the pornography site. The virus also hacked the unsecure e-mail lists and distributed pornography to the recipients on the list, many of whom were minors.

The church fired the young technologist. But the shame stuck with the kid for a long time. Everyone in the church understood the situation, but first-time visitors weren't as understanding. One of them who received a pornographic e-mail from the church's account alerted the press, and they had a field day. Before the church could correct the problem, the local paper ran a news story with the headline "Church Distributes Pornography." This paper pummeled the church, and it never recovered. The school closed its doors for good, and the church might as well have done the same, considering how the attendance dropped off.

〜

Minding His Business Basic Principle:

Treat your database like you treat cash. The fewer people who touch it, the better.

CHAPTER 40

YOU WILL KNOW THEM BY THEIR FRUIT

I once worked with a ministry that had been started by one man and quickly grew into a megachurch. The pastor was driven and smart—probably one of the most intelligent people I've ever met. Whenever somebody asked him how he'd managed to build such a huge ministry, he would answer, "By executing brilliant ideas."

He would go on to say, "A brilliant idea is worth a nickel. Executing that idea and turning it into reality is where real value is created." This pastor understood that talk is cheap. He knew that a ministry that talks more than it accomplishes will struggle to grow. He also knew that productive people produce measurable results, or output. You can see the "fruit" of their labor.

Deciding what to do is easy; figuring out how to execute it is far more difficult, but it's the "how" that gets things done. Thus, answering this question is the most important step in starting a new project.

One church I worked with had an aging congregation, and they were struggling to figure out a way to attract new, young families.

They could have asked themselves, "Why aren't we getting new families?" or "Who is getting new families, and how are they doing it?" Instead, they simply recognized their need and decided to hire a "family life minister."

Now, I need to digress for a moment. Hiring someone new is the easy answer. It's also the least cost-effective and the least creative, and requires the least managerial expertise. The thought process that leads to that decision usually goes something like this: We have a problem. None of us knows how to solve that problem. If we had someone on staff who knew how to solve the problem, we would not have that problem. Let's hire someone to solve the problem.

Problem solved...right?

Not always. Many times, managers believe that they've "hired" the solution to the problem, when all they've really done is passed off a tough problem to the new guy. Worst of all, during the hiring process, they neglect to ask the candidates how, specifically, they would fix the problem, and how they've fixed similar problems in the past.

Back to my story. The church put out a search and received all kinds of resumes. One candidate was currently working as a "family life minister." They brought him in and questioned him about the church where he worked. It was much larger than theirs, so they were impressed. When they asked him, "What does 'family life ministry' look like to you?" he talked about dynamic children's programs, family Bible studies, and people helping one another. He cast a vision of what it would look like "when we're successful."

I was doing some other work for the church, and they asked me to conduct a final interview to confirm their inclination to hire him.

"Do you have a plan?" I asked him.

"Not yet," he said.

"Can you write up a plan for us?"

I asked this question fully knowing him to be incapable of writing up a plan, since he barely knew anything about the church. I figured that if he knew how to do the job, my request for a plan would produce many questions ("fruit") from him, and the nature of those questions would be a telling indicator of his experience in managing a family life ministry.

Instead, he said, "No problem."

This response concerned me a little, but I figured I would still find out what he did or did not know about leading.

A few days later, I received his "plan"—basically a typed-up version of what he'd told the interviewers a few days earlier. According to his "plan," family ministry would have a dynamic children's program, small groups, volunteer opportunities, and so forth.

"That's not a plan," I pointed out.

"What do you mean?"

"If you watched a video recording of a day in the life of a children's minister, and there was no sound, what would you see?"

"Children having fun," he replied.

"Okay, then what would a day in the life of a family life minister look like?" I pressed him. "How will you recruit volunteers? Who will write to them? Who will call them? How will you handle announcements during services? How far in advance do you have to get things done? What will it cost?"

He couldn't answer any of my questions. I advised the church leadership against hiring him. They hired him anyway and never did get a plan from him. After two years, they finally let him go, while the church congregation kept aging and attendance kept declining.

Someone first should have asked why they were not attracting young families. If a family life pastor was the solution, then someone should have asked the candidate how he was going to get it done. Has the candidate ever encountered similar challenges before and how did he/she overcome those challenges?

A smaller church had the same problem—it couldn't attract any new young families. Someone on the leadership team had a different solution. He said, "Young people like technology, and we don't have a Web site." (By the way, Web sites are important; 57 percent of people who claim no church affiliation visited a church Web site in the last twelve months.)

The church's youth pastor had developed a small Web site for the youth group, so the leadership team asked her to build one for the church. They had no communication strategy, no marketing plan, and no budget. It took her almost a year to "build" the site, which was little more than a collection of blog pages. The landing page featured two buttons: one that said, "Click here if you are a member," and another that said, "Click here if you are not a member." (You can't make this stuff up.)

The common error of thought in many churches is, *If we build it, they will come.* It's not so much the "what" of the Web site that is important as it is the "how": How you will maintain it? How will you ensure that the content is up-to-date? How you will drive traffic to it? How will you capture the contact information of site visitors? How will you produce fresh content? And so on.

After about a year, the church contacted my company and asked us to build them a "new" new Web site. We worked with them to arrive at a reasonable strategy that they could maintain without undue costs, and then we built them a site. We also provided a marketing and communication strategy that was feasible for them to execute. They are now seeing the fruits of our efforts: 8,000 hits a month from over 5,000 unique users per year. And many young families have joined the church.

⁓

Minding His Business Basic Principle:

Before you decide on what you are going to do, spend some time considering how you are going to do it and how you will keep it going.

CONCLUSION

If you read one thing in *Minding His Business* that will make your life of service easier, then my prayers have been answered, and this book has served its purpose. As I said at the outset, there are very few "new problems," just new people having the "same old problems," usually for the same reasons and requiring the same solutions. In these pages, I've discussed some of them. But together, we can solve a lot more.

Christians are mandated by Christ to go and make disciples. In the first three centuries of the church, the process of "going" and "making" required that the religious leaders stay focused on the things of God while leaving the administrative and executive elements of ministry to people better suited to those tasks. We see a perfect example of this in Acts 6:1–4:

> *In those days when the number of disciples was increasing, the Hellenistic Jews among them complained against the Hebraic Jews because their widows were being overlooked in the daily distribution of food. So the Twelve gathered all the disciples together and said, "It would not be right for us to neglect the ministry of the word of God in order to wait on tables. Brothers and sisters, choose seven men from among you who are known to be full of the Spirit and wisdom. We will turn*

this responsibility over to them and will give our attention to prayer and the ministry of the word."

Today, there is a plethora of consultants and church growth experts ready to offer a universe of new techniques and turnkey plans to help pastors and ministry leaders "get to the next level." Many of their ideas are workable, but I would recommend that you first ask, "Do we need a new idea?" When it comes to "making" disciples, is there any replacement for a called man or woman leading God's people as they "go"? In business—church or otherwise—it isn't always the "best" idea but the best *execution* of an idea that wins the day.

You don't have to be a church growth expert to recognize that the church is in danger of losing relevance in an increasingly secular culture. Each year, a smaller and smaller percentage of people in the West claim Christ as their Lord and Savior. In fact, as I write, the fastest-growing religious demographic in the United States is that of people who claim no religious affiliation at all. And this is increasingly true of the younger generations. Is there anyone one better suited for engaging the secular culture than those men and women whom God has called into ministry? Then why would we ask these pastors, evangelists, and musicians to administrate and manage the business of the church, on top of their already demanding duties? Why would we ask them to perform tasks for which, in all likelihood, they have no training? It is a recipe for burnout and failure.

Minding His Business was written to help pastors and ministry leaders become free from the never-ending waterfall of details and disappointments that is often involved with management and administration. It was written also to help Christian businesspeople serve the church in order to free pastors and leaders to fulfill the Great Commission.

If you have a "stone in your shoe" for which you cannot find a solution from these pages, please feel free to contact me. I have spent years as a trusted voice of reason to pastors and ministry leaders as I help them navigate the organizational and business challenges facing them. The Provisum Group conducts church business every day for many leaders. I surrendered my life to this purpose years ago and joyfully serve pastors and ministry leaders in obedience to God. Please test me on this.

As you walk out the principles I've provided in these pages, my prayer is that you will reach more people with less hassle, and you'll be blessed in everything you set your hand to. I would love to hear how you are doing! Just write me at Don@TheProvisumGroup.com.

ABOUT THE AUTHOR

Don Corder's calling is to make the world a better place by serving the people who make the world a better place. He has dedicated his life to easing the burden of pastors and ministry leaders by improving the management and administration of church business. The church is filled with passionate lovers of people leading others in service. But passion will only get us so far. Eventually, getting the job done that God has called His church to do, includes raising money, managing resources, leading people, hiring staff, and communicating pastoral vision.

Don's career is highlighted by over thirty years of success in executive leadership with for-profit and nonprofit organizations, churches, and ministries. He currently leads The Provisum Group, a Christian nonprofit dedicated to setting church leaders free by managing the business of the churches and ministries they lead. The Provisum Group does this by putting systems in place that allow the ministers and other staff to serve their congregations and their communities without having to deal with the challenges of church management and administration.

Don is a trusted advisor to pastors and ministry leaders in the areas of church business administration, marketing, and management. With a natural ability to turn vision into reality, he is results-oriented with a unique blend of spiritual maturity, leadership skills, and analytical abilities, as well as a broad base of experiences. He has decades of experience helping churches and other nonprofits conduct their business with passion and prudent management, in congregations as small as 100 and as big as 12,000 with budgets as small as a few hundred thousand dollars to over $50 million.

Don and his wife, Jill, have been married for over thirty years. They have three grown sons and reside in central Ohio.

Welcome to Our House!

We Have a Special Gift for You

It is our privilege and pleasure to share in your love of Christian books. We are committed to bringing you authors and books that feed, challenge, and enrich your faith.

To show our appreciation, we invite you to sign up to receive a specially selected **Reader Appreciation Gift**, with our compliments. Just go to the Web address at the bottom of this page.

God bless you as you seek a deeper walk with Him!

WHITAKER
HOUSE